Modernism in Focus

by
Lucien Jenkins

Also available from Rhinegold Publishing:
Romanticism in Focus
Baroque Music in Focus
Madonna in Focus
Who's Next in Focus
Batman in Focus
Goldfinger in Focus

Rhinegold Study Guides

Students' Guides to GCSE, AS and A2 Music for the AQA, Edexcel and OCR Specifications
Listening Tests for GCSE, AS and A2 Music for the AQA, Edexcel and OCR Specifications

A Student's Guide to GCSE Music for the WJEC Specification
A Student's Guide to Music Technology for the Edexcel AS and A2 Specification
Listening Tests for Students: Edexcel AS and A2 Music Technology Specification

A Student's Guide to AS Classical Civilisation for the AQA Specification

Students' Guides to AS and A2 Drama and Theatre Studies for the AQA and Edexcel Specifications

Students' Guides to AS and A2 Performance Studies for the OCR Specification
Students' Guides to AS and A2 Religious Studies for the AQA, Edexcel and OCR Specifications

Rhinegold Publishing also publishes Classical Music, Classroom Music, Early Music Today, Music Teacher, Opera Now, Piano, The Singer, Teaching Drama, British and International Music Yearbook, British Performing Arts Yearbook, Rhinegold Guide to Music Education, Rhinegold Dictionary of Music in Sound.

First published 2007 in Great Britain by
Rhinegold Publishing Ltd
241 Shaftesbury Avenue
London WC2H 8TF
Telephone: 020 7333 1720
Fax: 020 7333 1765
www.rhinegold.co.uk

© Rhinegold Publishing Ltd 2007

Modernism in Focus
British Library Cataloguing in Publication Data.
A catalogue record for this book is available from the British Library.
ISBN: 978-1-906178-14-7
Printed in Great Britain by Thanet Press

Contents

The author

Lucien Jenkins is the author of a series of poems titled *Laying out the Body* (Seren Books) and *Romanticism in Focus* (Rhinegold 2007), and co-author of the *Classical Music Encyclopedia* (Collins 2000). His edition of the *Collected Poems* of George Eliot was praised by Gillian Beer in the *Times Literary Supplement*. His editions of *The Necromancer* by Peter Teuthold and *The Midnight Bell* by Francis Lathom (two of the gothic novels cited in Austen's *Northanger Abbey*) were welcomed by *The Year's Work in English Studies*. His book with CDs for Naxos *Discover Early Music* was called a 'clear, well-informed introduction... In dealing with more complex forms, Jenkins excels. He lays out just enough information to make the general listener aware of the kinds of things that are happening without going into intimidating detail' (All Music Guide). He is also the editor of the *Rhinegold Dictionary of Music in Sound* (Rhinegold Publishing 2001) and *The Illustrated Musical Instruments Handbook* (Flame Tree 2006).

He studied for his BA at Cambridge University, and for his MA and PhD at London University. He has taught for Ruskin College, Oxford, the Open University and Bristol University's lifelong learning department. He is a former member of the board of the Poetry Society, and has worked as a reviewer, critic and journalist for history, literature, dance, music and the visual arts. He was a member of the Qualifications and Curriculum Authority's Music Development Group (helping rewrite the music content of the National Curriculum), and has been a judge in the Classic FM Music Teacher of the Year since its inception. He is the former editor of *Music Teacher*, and the founder of *Early Music Today*, *Classroom Music* and *Teaching Drama*.

The editors

Ben Robbins, Sophie Buchan, Rose Vickridge, Chris Elscombe.

Acknowledgments

The author and publishers wish to thank Pamela Lidiard, Hugh Benham and John Walker for their advice during the preparation of this book.

Cover images (top to bottom): © Tate, London 2007
© Kritian Sekulic
© Bernice Abbott/ Commerce Graphics Ltd

Preface

Cultural historians tend to use a set of six overarching terms to describe and categorise all European art forms since the ancient world: Medieval, Renaissance, Baroque, Classical, Romantic and Modern. In each case, the name specifies a period in which cultural practice is markedly different from that of the previous age. The differences are pronounced in every art form, and these differences are, to a certain extent, interrelated across all art forms. Thus there is something about the Renaissance, for example, which its painting, sculpture, literature and music all share and reflect.

This is not to say that there is not a rich vocabulary of other cultural-historic terms, but they each tend to be limited to a specific decade, art form, group or country. For example, in this book you will also encounter the following terms: Cubism, Expressionism, Fauvism, Futurism, Imagism, Impressionism, Naturalism, Neoclassicism, Pre-Raphaelite, Realism, Surrealism and Symbolism.

In order to start thinking about Modernism, we need to shape an understanding of what it is and what it isn't. We also have to consider when and where it originated. But rather than discussing this in abstract terms, it will be more beneficial to examine a specific work from a specific moment in cultural history. Schnitzler's play *La Ronde* is a **transitional** work and a clear example of incipient Modernist thought and practice. Originally published under the title *Reigen*, it sparked demonstrations and a prosecution for its author, but has subsequently been staged, translated, filmed and televised. Dating from 1900, it possesses four recognisable literary qualities of the 19th century:

> The concept of 'transitional' is a rewarding one in itself; figures include Thomas Hardy, Joseph Conrad and W. B. Yeats; Gustav Mahler, Richard Strauss, and Erik Satie; Paul Cézanne, Gustav Klimt and Gustave Moreau.

1. Its cast of characters are part of a society that the audience would understand as its own – husbands, wives, soldiers, maids – and shows them experiencing recognisable emotions such as excitement, desire and embarrassment.

2. It tackles the traditional theme of temptation.

3. It explores the key 19th-century topic of the interwoven nature of society, a theme that can be found in the work of Dickens, Balzac and countless other novelists.

4. It employs a mimetic approach to the everyday world, typical of realist and naturalist novelists and playwrights, with recognisable speech patterns (including variations to match characters' gender, age and social class) and

familiar everyday topics of conversation, thus inviting a staging where the clothes and setting are typical of the age.

On the other hand, four clear aspects of this play do anticipate Modernism:

1. It deals directly with sexuality, as every scene shows a couple in love or a flirtation, and every scene ends with sexual intercourse. An implicit theme is sexually transmitted disease. Schnitzler, himself a practising doctor, shows how marriages, affairs, flirtations and professional liaisons between men and women ensure that any disease contracted by a prostitute will find its way to well-to-do ladies and gentlemen who have never visited her. This is clearly a development of the 19th-century theme of the interconnectedness of society, but develops this theme in an area of life and society that no novelist of the earlier period would have tackled so directly.

2. There is no explicit plot. One character from each scene's couple is to be found in the next scene, giving the play a sense of unifying and progressive structure, but there is no sense of a story which each scene develops and takes forward in the way that there is in Ibsen's *Ghosts*, for instance.

> This structure is what gives the play its name, for a 'ronde' is a kind of dance in which partners change. Schnitzler may also expect us to notice that these encounters, though some are serious relationships, others flirtations or commercial transactions, are treated with equal validity, so that we question the manner in which men and women relate.

3. A key aspect of late-19th-century plays, especially those of Ibsen and Chekhov, was character development. In *La Ronde*, however, we do not get to know anyone; just as there is no plot, there is also no context in which to develop characters who have already been reduced to impersonal social functions ('the soldier', 'the maid'). Their status in society is foregrounded, but we know nothing of their childhood, their ambitions, their secrets or their complexities. These are characters in the same way that the pilgrims in Chaucer's *Canterbury Tales* or Bunyan's *Pilgrim's Progress* are characters. They fulfil a purpose in the play, but the play is not about them.

4. *La Ronde* is constructed from a sequence of short self-contained scenes. There are no long interconnected acts where characters arrive and depart, no plots and subplots to interweave and mutually enlighten one another.

Just as there are aspects of the play which we can trace back to a great deal of 19th-century and earlier literature, so there are clearly things that are new. These features – the concern with **sexuality and morbidity** and the **disruption of the traditional structures of the genre** – characterise a surprisingly large number of Modernist works in several art forms.

> The emphasis on morbidity as a mark of Modernism was anticipated by Romantic works, such as Puccini's *Tosca* (1887) and much of Baudelaire's poetry.

These two aspects may seem divergent, but they are in fact connected. Modernist artists shared a conviction that the previous several decades had been marked by a collective apathy on the part of artists and audiences, a tacit agreement whereby nothing unexpected or controversial was mentioned. Modernism, by calculated contrast, denotes a commitment to upsetting, disturbing and challenging audiences. That challenge may be present in its choice of topic (nothing upset an audience at that time more than the subject of human sexuality), or by the way in which the work tells or refuses to tell a story. We shall also see that there were painters, playwrights, novelists and other cultural figures who may not really count as Modernists, but who nevertheless set out to shock audiences and readers, shatter artistic complacency and force people to analyse their own role as cultural consumers.

This is not to say, however, that the 19th century did not see stirrings of artistic revolt. Consider the references to the Pre-Raphaelites and Symbolists in Pound's *Mauberley*. Also, the situation in France was not identical to that in Britain (see page 13).

1
The historical context

Europe at the beginning of the 20th century had been profoundly marked by the twin phenomena of imperialism in politics and Romanticism in art. And although it is a mistake to think of a work entirely as the product of its times – since factors such as the life of the artist and the art's own internal logic must be taken into account – it is true to say that any work is, to a certain extent, shaped by its surroundings.

Romanticism

Romanticism was the dominant aesthetic of the 19th century and, as such, it not only shaped every art form of the day but also profoundly affected the way that people lived their lives. Romanticism is just as awkward to define and tie down to a single unified meaning as Modernism. But certain aspects of it can be listed:

For more on Romanticism, see *Romanticism in Focus*, Lucien Jenkins (Rhinegold 2007).

- There is a concern with **childhood** and a belief in its spiritual, creative and religious importance. The Romantics believed that adult human beings were not merely the extension of their smaller, younger selves, but the product of their childhoods. In Wordsworth's words, 'the child is father to the man'.
- Romantic work demonstrates a new and different relationship with **nature**. Where once nature was simply a useful storehouse from which human labour could derive food and materials, in the Romantic period it came to be regarded as something possessing an inherent aesthetic and moral value. Nature is divine, and contemplating it can open up a sensitivity to the ineffable and the transcendental, or, as it was termed, the 'sublime'. Poets and painters increasingly sought out wild landscapes rather than cultivated ones, in a search for the truths of nature and, by extension, the truths governing human nature.
- There was a belief in the centrality of **human** experience. The artists of previous centuries had worked within a framework whereby man lived in a *divinely* ordered universe and the majority of high art had been devoted to Christian worship. From the Renaissance onwards there was a growing emphasis on men and women's *earthly* lives.
- Out of this grew the Romantic notion of the **heroic individual**, a figure embodied in an artist such as Michelangelo or a soldier such as Napoleon. Romantic artists, such as Beethoven, Byron and Pushkin, began to be treated as heroic in their own right because the **artist** came to be awarded a far higher status than ever before. They were seen variously as prophets,

visionaries, revolutionaries or quasi-priests, and were clearly leaders and initiators of change, rather than mere entertainers. This was a process that began in the Renaissance where initially only writers were close to being respectable because of their proximity to scholars and clerics. However, this notion extended only gradually until composers, painters and others were admired by the educated classes, not merely hired as and when entertainment was required. This change is often referred to as the breakdown of the patronage system.

> The patronage system was the process by which the rich paid artists money. It meant that in various ways over the centuries artists' jobs included praising their employer. The Romantic movement saw artists aiming to be more financially independent and thus have greater freedom in their choice of subject, genre and critical stance.

- These factors combined to encourage composers to write louder works for larger orchestras, to make bigger melodic statements and to demand increasing virtuosity from performers. Instrument makers sought to create louder instruments and concerts took place in larger halls. In literature, the novel achieved such a dominant position that every other literary genre was forced to react by either imitating the novel or deliberately setting itself apart. The novel,

> Mahler talked about his Symphony No 8 in language which suggested it contained an entire solar system; Skryabin called for his unrealised opus *Mysterium* to be performed in the foothills of the Himalayas.

like the symphony, grew larger both in size and ambition, as both sought to represent an entire world, to show the whole of a society or the whole of a human soul.

Continuity and change

As you begin to know and understand more about Modernism's ambitions, you may decide that it was really only a reinvented version of Romanticism. For example, voices in both movements claimed that poetry should be written in real, everyday language and rescued from the artificial style of the preceding literary period. This is in part because the Romantic style had itself crystallised into a new academic approach, which was applied without thought or examination by many professionals and amateurs, who were merely following a set of rules.

The arch-Modernist composer Arnold Schoenberg wanted to take music forward into new areas, despite his huge respect for composers like Bach, Beethoven and Wagner. Schoenberg saw tradition not as a limiting force but as a challenging one, writing not of rupture with the past, but rather of his need to possess and imitate what had gone before. Indeed he saw the process of assimilating his predecessor's styles as a prerequisite to creating a new music.

> 'National Music' in *Style and Life* ed. Leonard Stein, trans. Leo Black, (Faber, 1975).

Schoenberg believed that music was essentially a dramatic narrative, which demonstrated development and change, a constant pushing of boundaries, and a search for new worlds to explore. He was also very idealistic in his view of music's purpose, in that he believed it had a spiritual, almost religious mission. An arch-Romantic of the previous century such as Hector Berlioz would have had no difficulty with such a philosophy. Perhaps above all, artists continued to be seen as (and in part to present themselves as) heroic figures who should not be judged by ordinary human standards. Pablo Picasso is a prime example of this, and, in this respect, he is the descendant of Delacroix, Berlioz and Byron.

On the other hand there are certain marked differences that delineate the divide between Romanticism and Modernism. Modernism placed an emphasis on **urban** experience in a way that Romanticism did not. Modernist literature rarely yearns for the countryside even when presenting urban experience negatively. Unlike Modernism, Romanticism continually had recourse to the natural world because of a belief that mankind was mortal and earthly. Ravel's comment that he was 'naturally artificial' was deliberately intended to amuse and provoke, in the spirit of Oscar Wilde, but it is also a highly Modernist comment on the Romantic conception of the natural. It rather echoes the views on 'the simple and natural' expressed by George Knightley in Jane Austen's *Emma* (1816), written when Romantic ideas of Nature were just entering high fashion.

Modernism also avoids solemnity. It can be both serious and comic, but avoids the pretentiousness that weighed down later Romanticism. Ezra Pound deliberately parodies not only his predecessors (Tennyson and Housman), but also his contemporaries (Rudyard Kipling and T. S. Eliot). Eliot's *Hollow Men* and *Sweeney Agonistes* both exhibit a sophisticated gallows humour. Stravinsky's *Golliwogg's Cakewalk* and *Ragtime*, and his acceptance of a commission to write a polka for circus elephants, are all examples of this rejection of pomposity.

As such, they anticipate Beckett's tragic-comic aesthetic. See page 48.

Similarly, Schoenberg quotes a popular song in his String Quartet No 2 and Bela Bartók writes a sneering imitation of a passage of Shostakovich's *Leningrad* Symphony into his *Concerto for Orchestra*. It is as if, despite the deep seriousness of their own work, Modernist artists were keen not to fall into the trap assuming the pomposity of their immediate predecessors, whereby the Romantic artist had become a humourless, heroic figure. They set out to deliberately stand outside society in order to criticise its hypocrisies.

Imperialism

Modernists actively sought out revolutionary new influences to help them break free of the aesthetic confines in which they believed their art forms to be imprisoned. For the first time in cultural histroy, non-European influences were of structural importance, becoming central to works of art. There are certain points of contact with foreign ideas that were of great significance to particular artists, where exposure both freed them from the formal restraints and cultural assumptions governing their art form and offered them a new level of insight into their own personal or creative challenges.

- Debussy first heard a Javanese gamelan at the 1889 Paris exhibition. Its influence is often pointed to in his String Quartet in G minor (the pizzicato in the Scherzo) and the ostinato in his 'Pagodes' from *Estampes*.

  > Gamelan is the traditional instrument and music of Indonesia, particularly of Bali and Java.

- Picasso came into contact with African art when he moved to Paris via the newly developing market in anthropological artefacts there.
- T. S. Eliot was intrigued by Indian philosophy and theology. The title of the third section of his *The Waste Land*, 'The Fire Sermon', is taken from Gautama Buddha's teachings and he tellingly interweaves quotations from it with lines from a late-Classical Christian book. He also quotes the Hindu scriptures, the Upanishads, in the final section of the poem.
- In W. B. Yeats' case, the study of Indian thought formed part of his wider explorations of esoteric philosophies. His autobiographical writings describe his search to find the spiritual roots of humanity that modern life (and recent literature) had lost touch with. He was influenced by a range of diverse figures, such as the theosophist Madame Blavatsky, the occultist Aleister Crowley and the Bengali poet Rabindranath Tagore.

This interest in non-European culture may have had its roots in the Romantic movement, one feature of which was a fascination with the bizarre and the macabre. But Modernism treated such material very differently. Romanticism had emphasised the foreign and strange in figures such as the Spanish Gypsies in Prosper Mérimée's *Carmen* and Victor Hugo's *Notre-Dame de Paris*.

> Gothic novels became bestsellers in Britain before Romanticism was launched as a poetic project, although some Romantic poets did read Gothic novels. Shelley was married to one of the most famous Gothic novelists, Mary Shelley, who wrote *Frankenstein*.

Modernism, however, abandons this focus on what critics often call 'local colour'. The non-European element, like the non-rational, does not merely decorate Modernist works, it causes a radical rethink, resulting in new subjects and new structures.

I use the word 'bizarre' here because it is part of Baudelaire's critical vocabulary ('Le beau est toujours bizarre'). Baudelaire is a central figure in French Romanticism, but he could be described as one of the leading lights of incipient Modernism.

The First World War

The First World War caused more people to suffer than any previous war. The war was a time of mechanical advancement as trains, cars, aeroplanes, machine guns and tanks became part of the war effort. This made people see technology in a new and less benevolent light, undermining the 19th-century assumption that progress, improvement and civilisation were humanity's destiny. The shock of the war was all the more extreme as no major conflict had taken place in Europe since the Congress of Vienna in 1815. For a century, European armies had only been deployed in their countries' distant empires, against less well-armed enemies, and with minimal impact on civilians at home. It is thus not surprising that our concept of 'war poetry', which dates from the First World War, is very different from that of previous centuries.

2
The idea of being modern

The aesthetics of revolt

The idea of calling a movement 'Modernism' may strike us as strange. Surely every artistic development or experimentation can be labelled, within its given time period, 'modern'? Every age sees something new in the arts, as it does in the fields of technology and science. But Modernism was marked by a specific and avowed attitude to novelty. In music,

> Musicians at the beginning of the Baroque period were clearly very conscious of change, as witnessed in the habit of referring to 'stile antico' (old Renaissance style) and 'stile moderno' (the modern style).

literature, architecture, painting, sculpture, dance, theology and philosophy, breaking with the past came to be seen as a criteria for cultural value in itself. The past, particularly the recent past, was identified with a loss of direction and energy. The 19th century, what we in Britain would call the Victorian Age, became synonymous with hypocrisy and reticence, with false values and cultural entropy. And so artists looked to different times and places for the excellence they declared lacking from their own; to the Renaissance, the Middle Ages, Classical Greece and, as we have seen, foreign cultures.

The Irish poet William Butler Yeats talks in his autobiographical *Reveries over Childhood and Youth* about his childhood enthusiasm for science, and later revulsion against the 'authority' of Victorian scientific theory. At the same time, he records his growing excitement with alternative world views, and particularly the folk tales and legends of his native Ireland. Yeats is not saying that the scientific discoveries of his day were mistaken, but rather that there are elements of human experience that science does not explain or clarify, and that research into physical phenomena will finally leave us convinced that there is more to us than can be discovered empirically. By contrast, in the folk tales he found a kind of alternative, subversive logic that he pursued all his life.

This process of devaluing and revaluing tradition, the casting aside of the work of recent decades, and the determination to find unknown, lost or marginalised traditions, was central to the 20th century, and one aspect of modern life that Modernists drew upon heavily.

However vital this upheaval was, the implications for cultural life were not entirely positive. Good work was often decried if it showed the influence of another artist in the same medium. Indeed, as an extension of its apparent hostility to tradition, Modernism also seems to have damaged people's attitude to artistic influence in general. Pupilage, a process which every previous age accepted, has been criticised to such an extent by Modernism that many artists have ended up trying to be a school of one and carve out their own artistic tradition independently.

New influences

As part of the quest for an alternative logic, the Modernist project embraced playfulness and drew on the commedia del'arte. Schoenberg and Stravinsky shared an interest in the inheritance of commedia del'arte. As we saw in Chapter 1 (page 10), Modernism can be both serious and comic, but avoids the solemnity that weighed down later Romanticism. One of Schoenberg's most famous works from his Expressionist period is *Pierrot Lunaire* which describes the moon-struck loves and views of the stock character Pierrot. The French poet Jules Laforgue probably makes the most sustained reference to the commedia del'arte, and his poetry had a direct influence on T. S. Eliot's *Love Song of J. Alfred Prufrock*, with its ineffectual lover. Stravinsky's *Petrushka* has as its central character the eponymous puppet, who, though based on puppet shows at Russian Shrovetide fairs, draws on the commedia del'arte figure of Pulcinella.

> Commedia del'arte was an Italian theatrical tradition dating from the Renaissance that exploited stock roles, predictable comic storylines and masks.

> In Stravinsky's work, Petrushka's failed love, and contrast with the man of action, the Moor, also ally him closely with Pierrot.

References to masks and masked balls are to be found again in both Debussy's piano *Suite bergamasque* and Fauré's *Masques et Bergamasques*. It is not difficult to see the appeal of masks for the Modernists, since they can both disguise and dramatise identity, and thus perform a key dialectic between affectation and reality. Moreover, masks question the assumption that identity is simple and singular, suggesting its complex and polymorphous nature; one can assume a range of masks or identities, but none of these must be, or can be assumed to be, an authoritative representation of the self.

Another defining feature of Modernism is an emphasis on moonlight: *Pierrot Lunaire* translates as 'Pierrot under the influence of the moon'. Here, night is more than simply a period of the day, it is also indicative of disrepute. If daytime represents work and society, then night evokes notions of sexuality and criminality. Modernist works of art tried to draw attention not only to the inadequacy of daytime reason, but also to the importance of embracing night's irrationality. This is a shift evidenced in Joyce's work as he moves from *Ulysses*, a dawn-to-dusk novel, to *Finnegans Wake*, which takes place at nighttime.

These themes were explored by the mid-19th-century generation of French poets who bridged the gap between Romanticism and Modernism, as the world of Hugo and Gautier led to that of Baudelaire, and then on to Rimbaud and Mallarmé. The fact that English poetry never experienced this kind of progressive and incremental development was what made *The Waste Land* such a shocking departure from the poetry which had come before.

It is also important to notice that works can be modern without being Modernist. Evelyn Waugh wrote what may have been the first English novel to contain telephone conversations, but his novels were all written with essentially the same

13

narrative tools as had been used for a century or more. Edith Sitwell and her brothers deliberately set out to write works that turned the assumptions of Georgian poetry on their head. For example, where there was a highly successful series of anthologies called *Georgian Poetry*, they set up a rival called *Wheels*. The 'wheels' are

> Although relatively old-fashioned in his approach to narrative, Waugh was certainly aware of Modernism, taking the title and epigraph of *A Handful of Dust* from *The Waste Land*.

clearly emblematic of urban, mechanised life, and the title declares that while Georgian poetry was marked by its frequent references to landscape, rural traditions, country life and a sense of reassuring continuity, the Sitwells were in search of something anti-traditional, startling and inorganic.

But this hostile, antagonistic attitude to the arts does not achieve anything in itself. Pound, Stravinsky, Picasso and the other Modernist masters were not merely trying to startle audiences, attract column inches or make a social splash among the moneyed classes. They were trying to create a new form of art that valued experimentation. Perhaps that is why the British critic F. R. Leavis savagely dismissed the Sitwells

> *New Bearings in English Poetry*, F. R. Leavis, Chatto and Windus, 1950.

as belonging 'to the history of publicity, rather than of poetry'. It was obvious to T. S. Eliot that Osbert Sitwell was writing deliberate imitations of his own style, once Eliot's work became fashionable. Although he remained on friendly terms with him, Eliot went out of his way to ensure that people knew whose was the original work and who had written the copies. The true revolutionaries could see that what they were doing should not be seen alongside other work that was fashionable at the time (produced by 'third-rate and vulgar imitators'), but with the great work of other eras

> T. S. Eliot, *Collected Letters*, vol 1, p 573.

and other styles, including the 'really respectable and serious writers' of the older generation.

Was Modernism the only show in town?

We should also take note of the fact that Modernism was not the only cultural force shaping the 20th-century arts movement. Many composers, painters and writers continued to employ an essentially 19th-century Romantic idiom, and some composers, including Puccini and Vaughan Williams, continued to produce accomplished work following the rules of tonal systems.

> It should, however, be remembered that Vaughan Williams, a pupil of Ravel, did work with modality at some points and Puccini's later music showed that he was aware of the new sonorities being explored by younger composers.

D. H. Lawrence is one of the great novelists of the first half of the 20th century, but his narrative technique could be understood by readers familiar only with Flaubert and George Eliot. However, in dealing with relationships so much more directly and explicitly than his predecessors, he challenged previous representations of sexuality. *Lady Chatterley's Lover*, *The Rainbow* and *Women in Love* tackle the subjects of heterosexuality and homosexuality, marriage and adultery, love and friendship, and the spiritual and the physical facets of relationships, with a directness and frankness that was unattempted by 19th-century novelists.

The development of the intensely felt Modernist art form, Expressionism, clearly mirrors the strain which society and individuals were under at the time of the First World War. But not all artists chose this style to express their response to social duress. Siegfried Sassoon, who was decorated for bravery in the war, wrote a number of savagely funny, bitterly angry lyrics condemning the complacency of British society at home and the callousness of an incompetent officer class. His achievement is to imbue these poems with intense emotion while retaining complete clarity of language. As a result, a readership which might have rejected what they perceived as Modernist pretentiousness had to face the fact that here was a poet who could pass all the old-fashioned tests of poetry, those of harmony and clarity, just as they had to accept that this was the voice of a decorated veteran (he had been awarded the Military Cross) who was publicly condemning the war and its conduct.

For Expressionism in music, see page 19.

Ralph Vaughan Williams wrote his Symphony No 3 in the immediate aftermath of the war. Although a later composer dismissed it as 'cowpat music' the intention of the work was to dramatise how much the war had destroyed. This work was in a sense a eulogy, since Vaughan Williams had lost his friend, the composer George Butterworth (1885–1916), in the Battle of the Somme. The older Edward Elgar had originally supported the war, as most patriots did, but his 1919 cello concerto sounds like an extended lament, an *In Memoriam* for a world irrevocably destroyed. And so while Sassoon, Vaughan Williams and Elgar wrote wonderful music and poetry at the time that Modernism was 'happening', they were not quintessentially Modernist themselves.

Symphony No 3 was first performed in 1922. This was a significant year for Modernist art since *The Waste Land* and *Ulysses* were both published.

A vast amount of narrative and dramatic literature written, published and broadcast on radio, television and film, shows little influence of Modernism. When some of Samuel Beckett's work for television was broadcast, at least one reviewer was struck, perhaps for the first time, by the extent to which television was dominated by realism. The screenwriter Dennis Potter (1935–1994), however, was vitriolic in the hostility of his response to Beckett's work. The playwright Edward Bond (b. 1934), similarly committed to an essentially realistic aesthetic, has also been critical of Beckett's plays. Both criticised Beckett's supposed refusal to deal with reality, that is, with recognisable public and private subjects such as wars and divorces. In fact, an attentive audience can

For more on Beckett, see page 48. Bond's politics affected his critical judgement. See page 46 for a discussion of 'engagé' art.

15

find that Beckett's dramas do indeed deal with such things, but at a level and from an angle that abstract direct commentary.

Radio, however, has enjoyed a more varied range of drama. Its soap operas are as staid as those of television, but its plays have included works by Beckett (*All That Fall*), Plath (*Three Women*) and Thomas (*Under Milk Wood*).

3
Modernism in music

By the end of the 19th century, composers such as **Gustav Mahler** and **Anton Bruckner** (1824 – 1896) were creating an orchestral sound which drew heavily on that of Wagner. In their quest to convey the emotional and spiritual depths of human experience these composers were already pushing tonal systems to their limits. Mahler married simple folk tunes with rich chromaticism, triumphant brass fanfares with bitter funeral marches, creating an effect which was both heroic and sardonic. In doing so he wrote the most philosophically challenging music of his age.

Mahler was born 200 years after the orchestra's conception and those 200 years had seen the orchestra become the most important ensemble in Western art music. It had also grown in size, in terms both of the number of players and the variety of instruments on stage. Richard Strauss' *Till Eulenspiegel* (1895) required 22 different types of instrument, including a string section of 64 players. In the hands of a master like Mahler, these vast orchestral forces could be balanced successfully with the lightness of a string quartet. But the threat, certainly among other composers, was that the music would collapse under the weight of its own scale and pretensions.

> Schoenberg's early work *Gurrelieder* is similarly gigantic; take a look at the score and start counting instruments.

The breakdown of rules

The idea of pushing artistic boundaries to extremes is one of the central tenets of Modernism. In his *Verklärte Nacht* op 4 (1899, first performance 1902), **Arnold Schoenberg**

> *Verklärte Nacht* means 'transfigured' or 'illuminated night'.

takes the harmonic language of Romanticism and pushes it until it begins to fall apart. The majority of Baroque, Classical and Romantic music since the middle of the 17th century had been written in a major or minor key. Composers had, however, added harmonic interest by writing in accidentals. These provided localised excitement and tension, as a sound that logically ought not to be heard suddenly intrudes, and the ear can either feel the unexpected rightness of the harmony, or witness the music cope with this invading force and restore the tonal order.

> Accidentals are sharps or flats which do not appear in the key signature but which are added individually to affect a specific note in a specific bar.

In *Verklärte Nacht*, a string sextet (Schoenberg later arranged the piece for string orchestra), there are so many accidentals that it is hard to be sure exactly which key the piece is in (it's actually D major/ D minor). It is in works like this that the music is breaking so many rules that the audience is left wondering why the rules were upheld in the first place. Prior to such revolutionary works, music had possessed, in its perfect, imperfect and other cadences, the equivalent of full stops and commas; a musical syntax. If the tonal home of a passage is unclear, then cadences will not function as they ought, causing an extreme disruption of musical language.

It is worth noting that *Verklärte Nacht* takes its title and programme from a poem by Richard Dehmel (1863–1920) which describes a man and a woman walking at night. In the poem, the woman confesses to the man that she is pregnant by another man. The music works through moods and themes of guilt, despair, forgiveness and ultimate transfiguration. Thus even instrumental music is tackling the question of human sexuality. Nor is the music's programme its only Modernist element. The strained quality of the music and its tonal vagrancy (as atonal music has no anchoring tonic) express the emotional and moral feeling of being lost, and are indicative of the Modernist motif of disorientation.

> A programme is an underlying plot which governs a piece of music. Programmes are found in Lieder, ballet, opera and film scores, but can also be found in purely instrumental, abstract music, as is the case here.

Expressionism

The music that grew out of the early Modernist period in Schoenberg's work is often termed Expressionist, and this is a term which is also applied to certain Modernist works in literature and the visual arts. The crucial element in Expressionist art across every medium is the artist's exploration of extreme emotional states. Although essentially tonal and Romantic, when viewed in the light of this definition, *Verklärte Nacht* already fits with the Expressionist paradigm. The Expressionist artist will push the boundaries of his medium to express emotional and spiritual strain. Schoenberg's music thus simultaneously reaches for an excessive richness of chromaticism and the kind of harmonic strains to be found in dissonances that seem to want to be resolved.

In painting, Expressionist works show distorted human beings externally manifesting the ugliness of their souls, while in literature, plays by writers such as Strindberg show people struggling with

> See also works by Barlach, Beckmann, Nolde and the Norwegian Edvard Munch.

marital breakdown and mental illness, yet moving towards some kind of spiritual insight. These artistic developments can be linked to the earlier music of Mahler and the plays of Ibsen. The plots of Ibsen's *Hedda Gabler* and *Ghosts* both anticipate the latent emotional tension of Expressionism, as does the desparate intensity of Mahler's music, but in both cases the intensity remains sufficiently contained to prevent the sense of the breakdown spreading to the works' larger formal structure. In fact, Mahler and Ibsen admired Schoenberg and Strindberg respectively. Ibsen recorded that in later life he had a picture of Strindberg on his study wall, as he could only write when 'that madman' was staring down at him.

Just as Expressionist painting favoured distortion and vibrant colour schemes, so Expressionist music frequently tended to demonstrate the following characteristics:

- Dissonance
- Violent changes of dynamics
- Violent changes of pitch and wide melodic leaps
- Sudden changes of texture
- Sudden changes of musical idea
- Instruments playing at the extremes of their ranges
- Chromatic harmonies.

The key non-technical words here are clearly 'violent', 'change' and 'extreme'. This is the music of a chaotic world in which the listener is afforded no position of tonal safety, such as:

- A home key
- Repetition
- Sequences
- Balanced phrases
- Cadences.

The latter characteristics, by contrast, imply the presence of a set of harmonic rules. The listener can learn these distinguishing features and by that means know how to map-read their way through a piece. They can enjoy, as in Romantic works, the moments when composers depart from the rules governing the piece. Expressionist art destroys the sense that we can control our responses to a work of art.

Schoenberg's *Pierrot Lunaire* is composed for female voice, piano, three strings and four woodwind – a non-standard, one-off ensemble. This instrumentation is in itself a deliberate statement of defiance, of an individual creative voice breaking free from traditional structures. The piece is consequently also a break from the language of musical logic. The singularity of the instrumentation is complemented by a revolution in vocal timbre. Schoenberg demanded a new way of singing which he named **Sprechgesang** ('speech-song'). Halfway between singing and speaking, Sprechgesang upsets our expectation of what a soprano should be doing, as well as leaving us unsure as to when she will be lyrical and when verbal. The piece contains a section labelled 'Valse de Chopin' in which the spoken text compares a Chopin waltz to a drop of blood that stains the lips of a dying person. The passage is accordingly in waltz time, $\frac{3}{4}$, but its angular melody and dissonant harmony are very far from anything the early Romantic Chopin would have chosen to write.

> You may also come across the corresponding Sprechstimme ('speech-voice').

> *Schoenberg: Pierrot Lunaire,* Jonathan Dunsby and Julian Rushton, CUP.

Schoenberg's pupil Alban Berg (1885–1935) also explored Expressionism in works such as his opera *Wozzeck*. In this work, a man who is being used as the subject for a scientific experiment gradually descends into insanity, murdering his adulterous lover and ultimately committing suicide.

The play from which he took the opera's story is *Woyzeck* by Georg Büchner (1813–1837). Büchner was an extremely anachronistic figure in German literature, anticipating by almost a century Modernism's fragmentation of form and emphasis on the darker recesses of the human psyche.

This emphasis on violence and extremes of emotion should not, however, lead you to believe that Expressionist composers dispensed entirely with aesthetic considerations. Certainly, Schoenberg's op 11 *Three Piano Pieces* and second string quartet, or Berg's violin and chamber concertos, or Strauss' *Salomé* have shocked audiences accustomed to the sonorities of music after Haydn and before Sibelius, as none of these pieces are delicate in the nature. But they are nevertheless hauntingly beautiful and possess an immense emotional power.

In all these cases, the underlying theme is that the *subject* of the work of art is so potent that it is capable of tearing the form of the work apart. This motif of self-annihilation extends to the idea that human beings, and by implication modern western society as a whole, are capable of tearing themselves to pieces. It is no coincidence that this aesthetic reflects many of the anxieties and troubles engendered by the First World War (1914–1918) and the Russian Revolution (1917).

Serialism

For a Classical mind, a world without rules is unthinkable. But even arch-Modernists found that, without the inherited constitution of tonality to obey or defy, the composing of extended instrumental works became problematic. As a result, Schoenberg and his circle tended, while composing in this atonal Expressionist idiom, to write either short works, works made out of short movements, or works that set a literary text, since the words gave them the armature they required.

Having presided over the transition from late-Romantic chromaticism to atonality and Expressionism, Schoenberg sought to develop a new musical practice. He found it in Serialism. Instead of adhering to tonality's choice of various notes as the tonic in various keys, which brings a sense of homecoming whenever that particular note recurs (so that a piece in C major will tend to end on C), Schoenberg chose to democratise notes, so that no note was more important than any other. The basis of a tonal work is the scale of the key in which the piece opens, and then those keys through which it passes. With a serial piece, the composer first writes out a 12-note melodic unit called a 'note row'.

Some critics have pointed to an apparent similarity between the development of equality among the 12 tones and the democratisation of language in poetry and prose which Gertrude Stein attempted at around the same time.

In a way, this combines the function of the scale with that of the 'theme', as in a series of variations upon a theme. The note row's first appearance is, logically enough, known as the 'prime'. Once it has been stated, it can come back in precisely the same form, or it can be reshuffled, so that the note *names* are retained in the same order as in the prime, but the actual *pitches* used are different. In addition, the prime can be run in reverse order (retrograde) or upside down (inverted), or a combination of the latter two (retrograde inversion). But the note row's recurrence gives the piece its coherence, both for the composer and the audience.

Arnold Schoenberg's String Quartet No 2 (1908) contains a quotation from a popular song of the time. At one point in the Scherzo, the second movement, the music quotes *Oh du Lieber Augustin*; specifically the passage which in the song says 'Alles ist hin', meaning 'It's all over', a musical declaration that previous musical codes of conduct are not just being suspended in this piece, they have actually ceased to have any useful meaning to Schoenberg whatsoever. This piece, although very beautiful, takes the listener on a journey from a tonal beginning to an atonal conclusion. Even the fact that a string quartet is joined by voice for the third and fourth movements would have been an unexpected development for its first audiences, since songs were usually written with a solo accompanist (at this time mostly a piano, but sometimes a guitar or other plucked instrument such as a mandolin).

Schoenberg was an admirer of Mahler, and this disconcerting quotation from a popular song in serious concert hall music is a very Mahlerian touch. It is an example of the blending of high and low art which is a defining characteristic of Modernism, part of its rejection of the high solemnity of late Romanticism. It is to be found elsewhere in Stravinsky's *Golliwogg's Cakewalk* and *Ragtime*. Modernist techniques were applied to popular subject matter to create a sophisticated new form of democratised entertainment.

Nationalism

As groundbreaking as the Modernists were, they did not advocate a complete rupture with older works of art, as composers frequently referenced pre-existing pieces and movements. Many late-Romantic composers, for instance, quoted from folk music, since one of the forms to which Romantic music turned was **nationalism**. The background to this is in part the nationalist and regionalist uprisings that took place in several parts of Europe, which in 1848 was still dominated by a handful of large empires. The lost political goal of self-determination translated into the artistic goal of self-definition. This gave a new purpose to the essentially Romantic idea of using the language of everyday life in poetry, as composers as different as Glinka, Sibelius, Vaughan Williams, Bartók, Grieg, Falla and Janácek sought out the lineage and folk inheritance of their local areas in order to create

Nationalism is usually treated as a musical period, like the Baroque; in fact, it is more like a political-cultural imperative which affected many composers, includes both late Romantics and Modernists.

an essentially regional musical style.

Later composers such as Bartók found that their folk music research led to the increasing use of the pentatonic scale and modes, scales which had been almost ignored for two centuries. Composers also explored other scales, such as the whole-tone scale which Debussy uses in 'Voiles' (*Préludes* book 1) and Ravel's string quartet. His use of the Phrygian mode in that quartet is a characteristic example of appealing to tradition (in the form of Beethoven's op 132), while still embarking on something radical. Such seemingly paradoxical approaches are often treated by music historians as divergent experiments. They do, however, all stem from a widespread discontent with what tonality seemed to have left to offer, and seek to weaken the tonal home. 'Voiles' and the Ravel quartet do not sound atonal, but the 'final' of a mode never has the magnetism of a scale's tonic, and a whole-tone scale inevitably sounds rather vague, so it is no wonder that Debussy chose the title of 'Sails' for the work.

> Beethoven's use of the Phrygian mode in his op 132 string quartet was unusual enough for him to feel the need to draw attention to it in his title.

> The title is a pun, as 'voile' also means 'veil' in French, with the implication of unclarity as well as floating. The way Debussy's music modulates without preparation also upsets the sense of tonal security.

The Rite of Spring

A similar motive to those outlined in the previous section lies behind **Igor Stravinsky's** composition of one of the defining works of Modernism, *The Rite of Spring* (1913). Sometimes it is hard to understand the fuss that surrounds the first performance of a work of art, but in the case of the *Rite* there is no mystery; the work is still startling today. Where other composers sought for a renewal of national self-definition in folk music, Stravinsky reached back to an imagined Stone Age and created the music for a ballet focused around a primitive fertility ritual where a young woman is sacrificed. The Modernist motifs of sexuality, violence and the extremes of human behaviour are immediately in evidence. The musicologist Adorno, who sought to analyse the ideas inherent in music, declared the *Rite of Spring* a necrophiliac work, on account of its focus on death. Schoenberg, although not a great fan of Stravinsky's, declared himself to be disgusted by the treatment of the Russian by a hostile public and critical establishment. The work employs dissonance to convey the brutality and inhumanity of a primitivistic ritual. Dissonance as such was nothing new; Mozart opened one of his string quartets with a dissonant passage and tonality in Beethoven's Symphony No 9 seems in frequent danger of breaking down. But when in the hands of Stravinsky it is turned from a localised effect into the structural purpose for an entire orchestral work.

> *Stravinsky: The Rite of Spring*, Peter Hill and Julian Rushton, CUP.

> In *Philosophie der neuen Musik*, 1949. See the *Cambridge Companion to Stravinsky* ed. Jonathan Cross, CUP 2003; Lorenz Jäger, *Adorno: A Political Biography*, Yale University Press 2004.

Just as the breakdown of tonality and increasing use of chromaticism in Romantic music is often linked to Wagner and specifically the *Tristan* chord, so for many critics, the touchstone of Modernism in music is the *Rite* chord. The *Tristan* chord, F−B−D♯−G♯, is a type of half-diminished 7th chord of ambiguous tonal identity. In other words, it's not clear which key it belongs to, leaving the listener unclear where the music is coming from and where it will go next, with all that implies about the primitivistic narrative and its directionless moral values. The music's excitement is derived in part from the anticipation of enlightenment, to see whether tonality can emerge from these mists in a satisfyingly heroic triumph over harmonic adversity.

In the section labelled 'Augurs of Spring', the *Rite* chord announces itself, seemingly compounding two different tonalities: an E♭ 7th chord is sitting on top of an F♭ chord. However, there are other ways of reading the *Rite* chord. We can interpret it as the product of an **octatonic scale**, and Stravinsky had certainly used an octatonic scale before, in *The Firebird* (1910) and in *Petrushka* (1911),

> An octatonic scale is an eight pitch-class scale which ascends in alternating steps of tones and semitones.

where it compounds C and F♯ major triads. Stravinsky would have encountered these when studying with his teacher Rimsky-Korsakov, who experimented with scales and traditional Russian sounds, and Stravinsky was clearly trying to evoke an ancient Russian tradition in this piece. This interpretation of the chord reminds us that the *Rite*'s 'tonality' is thus

> The best book on this is Richard Taruskin's *Stravinsky and the Russian Traditions*, Oxford 1996 but see also the *Cambridge Companion to Stravinsky* (ed.) Jonathan Cross, CUP 2003.

contemporary with Debussy's pentatonic scales and Balinese influence.

This idea of delving into folk culture in search of a pre-Christian cultural past is something Stravinsky shared with his contemporary, Yeats. As we noted in Chapter 2, the latter explored Indian religion, modern sects such as spiritualism and theosophy, and Irish folk tales. He did so in the context of a search for answers to the question of who human beings really are when you strip away the trappings of modern urban life that obscure and disguise individuals. Stravinsky's music implies that our concerns are rooted in sex, religion and violence, a sentiment echoed in the words of another contemporary, T. S. Eliot, where he reflects on the primacy of 'sex and copulation and death': *Sweeney Agonistes* (1932).

Just as the *Rite*'s harmonies challenged audiences and critics alike, so his use of **rhythm** dramatically departs from the recent past. For one thing, it is probable that no piece had previously been written in which an audience had been more aware of the percussion section. The off-beat rhythms he created were still unusual in classical music. In addition, the rapid changes of metre

> The presence of syncopation was well established in jazz.

effectively abolished the idea of a pulse. Where chromaticism had led to atonality and music where no one could be sure of the key signature, Stravinsky had written the first piece in which no one could work out the time signature. This is not to say that no one had ever changed time signatures before: Mussorgsky's

Pictures from an Exhibition switches between $\frac{6}{4}$ and $\frac{5}{4}$, but Stravinsky went beyond what anyone had expected. Most of the audience would have known music that had time signatures in multiples of two and three (e.g. $\frac{3}{4}$, $\frac{4}{4}$); dancing and walking beats. The *Rite* starts off with $\frac{3}{16}$, $\frac{2}{16}$, $\frac{3}{16}$, $\frac{3}{16}$, $\frac{2}{8}$, $\frac{2}{16}$, $\frac{3}{16}$, and has bars containing five, seven and 11 beats. Stravinsky also piles up several layers of conflicting ostinati (repeating patterns). It would have sounded not only unpredictable, but as unnatural as a body with a patternless heartbeat.

Furthermore, in other works (not the *Rite*, but certainly *Firebird* and *Petrushka*), Stravinsky reintroduced the piano to the orchestra after a century's absence. Throughout Romanticism, the

> There were a few exceptions such as Tchaikovsky's *Sleeping Beauty* and Saint-Saëns Organ Symphony, which includes a four-hands piano.

piano had been a chamber music, solo, Lieder and concerto instrument; since late Haydn it had rarely been a member of the orchestra. With Stravinsky and Schoenberg it came home, but it was used predominantly as a percussion instrument.

Nor was this the only surprise Stravinsky sprang in his orchestration. Another standard that every Romantic composer had taken for granted was the centrality and dominance of the strings. Every orchestral composer since Lully (1632–1687) had placed the violin, viola, cello and double bass sections at the heart of their orchestral writing. Gradually, through Classical and Romantic music, the number of wind instruments had increased, with clarinets, oboes, trumpets, trombones and so on finding a more central role. They began as single instruments adding a touch of colour to specific points in the piece, and during the 19th century they grew to acquire a force of their own, such as the central role of brass in Bruckner, for example. But in his *Symphonies of Wind Instruments* (1920), Stravinsky produced a piece in which there are no strings at all. The 18th century had known *Harmoniemusik*, but that had been light entertainment for outdoor

> This is a model which has influenced several composers including Olivier Messiaen (see page 51) and James MacMillan, who have written symphonic pieces in which the strings disappear for entire movements.

parties. A serious piece for a large mixed ensemble which excluded strings entirely was highly unusual – as were the harmonies Stravinsky wrote for ensembles. The contrast between the sprawling orchestras of late Romanticism and Modernism's affection for chamber orchestras is striking. Schoenberg's Chamber Symphony No 1 (1906) requires only 15 players. We have already looked at the orchestration of *Pierrot Lunaire*; other works to note in this context include Debussy's *Prélude à L'Après midi d'un faune*, Anton Webern's op 21 Symphony and Berg's Chamber Concerto, a double concerto in which the 'orchestra' accompanying the violin and piano soloists would certainly have surprised a 19th-century audience.

The *Rite* does contain strings, of course, but its opening is comprised of two minutes where only the woodwind play, two minutes of strings entries, then a further two minutes when only the woodwind play. Notice the high bassoon note that is the piece's first sound, right at the extreme of its tessitura. The *Rite* is a further example of the Modernist exploration of extremes; Stravinsky investigated how far an advanced instrumental technique could be taken, an exploration that marks much of avant-garde 20th-century music. Indeed a lot of new notational signs have had to be developed to score previously unknown effects, such as quarter tones, and some instruments have been damaged or even destoyed during such experiments.

See Otto Karolyi's *Introducing Modern Music*, Penguin 1995.

As well as wondering what happened to the time signature, the key signature and the bassoonist's concept of pitch, audiences found that their understanding of melody and melodic structures came under fire from Modernist forces. As early as 1894, a listener to Debussy's *Prélude à L'Après midi d'un faune* might well have felt that there wasn't a clear theme or melody that underwent a clear kind of variation or development, observes Christopher Butler. True enough, the piece seems fragmentary, unstable even, if you are depending on a theme-and-variations or first-subject-second-subject-development-section model to convince you a piece is observing a prescribed structure.

Cambridge History of 20th-Century Music, CUP, p 78.

If this melodic disruption or lack of clarity is analogous to any other artistic experiment, it the fragmentation of narrative in Modernist novels, which, in the case of Joyce, relies on the so-called 'stream of consciousness'. Here, Joyce moved closer to the way in which human thought patterns actually work, and that meant moving away from the grammar and syntax which are assumed to operate in conventional novels. It's all part of the Modernist commitment to disturbing the thought patterns of the audience, keeping them on edge and permanently unsure of what's coming next.

Before the *Rite*, the number of works of western art with the word 'spring' in the title are countless. Before Stravinsky, they had tended to emphasise the natural hopefulness implicit in renewed growth and sometimes were part of an allegory of the Christian notion of spring as allied to the Resurrection. In this piece there is nothing of the innocence of Beethoven's *Spring* sonata for violin and piano (op 24, 1801) or the pleasantness of Schumann's *Spring* symphony (op 38, 1841). Indeed, the audience famously rioted at the first performance,

The contrast parallels that between the opening of the *Waste Land* and that of the *Canterbury Tales*.

something attributable in part to the music, but perhaps more to the perceived obscenity and ugliness of the choreography. Nijinsky's emphasis on heaviness (tied to earth), itself dictated both by the composer's choice of subject and by the consequent percussive instrumentation, contrasted offensively with the lightness (escape from earth) which was what a ballet audience traditionally expected. This again takes us back to the revolutionary aspect of Modernism and the motive of making audiences listen to music with an alert mind, not seeing the arts as a means of escapism.

4
Modernism in Literature

Although various similarities can certainly be discerned between the different Modernist writers discussed in this chapter, you should also take note of their important differences. It is important to realise that belonging to a particular school or movement, being friends or contemporaries, does not make any two writers in any way identical.

Masks

The idea that when we present ourselves in company or to ourselves, we adopt an affectation to make certain conscious or unconscious impressions became a matter of fascination to the Modernist generation. They struggled with the idea of the unified self. Oscar Wilde had declared himself purely interested in the masks that people assumed. Part of a proto-modernist movement known as the 'Decadents', he had

> There were precedents to this Modernist concern; Schumann's attempts to understand his complex personality had driven him to develop three named and contrasting identities, the vigorous Florestan and the contemplative Eusebius, together with Meister Raro, whose task was to arbitrate between them. See his *Carnaval*.

made comic use of this interest in his play *The Importance of Being Earnest*, in which there is a non-existent character (Bunberry), and in which the hero, Jack Worthing, finally turns out to be the person he had been pretending to be for most of the play. Ezra Pound published an early volume of poetry

> Personae is the Greek and then Latin word for masks.

entitled *Personae*. Eliot's early work included several poems of medium length in which he adopted, like a novelist, the voices and personalities of various characters, in works such as Prufrock and the Lady in *Portrait of a Lady*, a title which clearly echoes that of Henry James' 1881 novel. Some reviewers, assuming that poetry was a personal medium, could not grasp that these 'voices' were no more the poet than David Copperfield was Dickens, complaining when Eliot appeared pretentiously to be calling himself an 'agèd eagle'(*Ash Wednesday*).

Eliot also adopted the role of an ineffectual, self-deprecating gentleman, failing to summon up the confidence to initiate a relationship. In this he emulates the poetic persona of Jules Laforgue, whose work he first encountered in 1908, through reading Arthur Symons's *The Symbolist Movement in Literature* (1895). Eliot's work began explicitly to declare the influence which French poets exercised over him. He quotes

> See the earlier discussion of masks and Laforgue, page 13.

Laforgue in 'Rhapsody on a Windy Night', for example. In *The Love Song of J. Alfred Prufrock* the narrator is an overtly Laforguian personality. In *The Waste Land*, the sequence of voices that interweave is a polyphonic extension of this

process. Donning a succession of masks allows Eliot to adopt a tone that is deliberately uncertain, both serious and playful, intimate and impersonal.

In the case of the Portuguese poet Fernando Pessoa, poems are attributed to four different names, only one of which is his own. The fiction of there being four independent poets is maintained in both the style and content of his poems: no one could be mistaken as to which 'author' wrote which poems. Nor was this fragmentation of the self merely a kind of highbrow joke: it was an essential element in allowing him to write. It is as if only by pretending to be a poet could he actually be one and write poems.

Paul Valéry (1871–1945) was a French poet with an enduring concern with the nature of identity. Twinned with this was a high degree of consciousness of the nature of language. Indeed, he declared that literature was a 'kind of extension and application of certain properties of language'. (Œuvres 1957, page 1441).

His *Fragments du Narcisse* is a long poem about the young man Narcissus and his experience of seeing his own reflection in a pool. It begins with a monologue by Narcissus who has just arrived at the water's edge. The second section addresses the fountain and contrasts the stories of love between couples that the peaceful spot has witnessed with his own loneliness. The final section considers the impossibility of union with the object of his own affections and ends with the destruction of the reflected image in an attempt at contact.

English readers will quickly become aware of something Keatsian in Valéry's work, with its use of internal rhyme and alliteration. Narcisse's declaration of solitude is an example of this in itself. But when structuralist critic Jonathan Culler draws attention to the euphony of the opening line of the sestet of his sonnet *La Dormeuse*, he suggests that the sound also encodes meaning: 'Dormeuse, amas doré d'ombres et d'abandon' ('sleeping woman, gilded heap of shadows and surrender'). Culler admits that we might be tempted to see it simply as a metaphor for the beauty of the sleeper (an idea familiar in English from Keats and Tennyson). But he goes on to say that the phonetic pattern 'Dor... doré, d'ombres, ...don' brings together a set of semantic elements (sleep, gold, shadows and gifts) and poses the possibility of their fusion.

Structuralist Poetics: Structuralist Linguistics and the Study of Literature, Jonathan Culler, RKP 1975.

Valéry returned to 'Narcisse' in his *Narcisse parle*. In addition, Salvador Dalí produced a characteristically startling version of the myth showing a pair of hands, one of which is turning into a kneeling figure. The young T. S. Eliot wrote two surviving Narcissus poems, one is now in his *Collected Poems* and was later recast and turned into a section of the *Waste Land*; the other is preserved in his *Collected Letters*. 'Narziß' occurs in Rilke's *Sonnette an Orpheus*, 'Spiegel: noch nie hat man wissend beschrieben' ('Mirror: no one has ever yet knowingly written about you') as well as Hesse's later *Narziß und Goldmund*, where he is the ascetic monk, contrasting with the younger more sensual pupil Goldmund ('Golden-mouth'). What made Narcissus so significant a figure for these prominent Modernists?

Perhaps the character fed into an implicit debate about the solipsism of Modernist works of art, with its reflection on the nature of creativity and questioning of the role of the artist. Sometimes neglected, sometimes working in isolation or as part of a small group of friends, Modernist artists could not have felt that they were engaged in the kind of public dialogue that Dickens, Hugo, Zola or even Tennyson understood as central to their work. When Valéry has Narcisse declare that 'Nulle des nymphes, nulle amie ne m'attire' ('none of the nymphs, no woman friend attracts me'), it is a Modernist declaration of the importance (or perhaps inevitability) of solitude.

But that line is also an acknowledgement that the poem traces its ancestry to Mallarmé's *L'Après midi d'un faune*, which had announced in its opening line, 'Ces nymphes, je veux les perpétuer'('These nymphs, I want to immortalise them'). In verse that is loyal to conventional prosody, he writes about the great poetic themes of mortality, the erotic and introspection. To English readers, his *Le Cimetière marin* (the cemetery by the sea) seems part of a tradition that we would trace to Gray's *Elegy Written in a Country Churchyard*, if not to the Lucretius whom Gray sometimes paraphrases. But his concluding stanza is enough to warn us that we are in danger of misreading him: 'Le vent se lève! … Il faut tenter de vivre!' ('The wind is rising! … We must strive to live!')

Valéry had known Mallarmé well in his youth, as well as Degas and Huysmans.

Rainer Maria Rilke (1875–1926) worked as secretary for a time to the French sculpture Rodin and critics have not been slow in pointing to this experience as an influence behind the poems collected in *Neue Gedichte* (*New Poems*). These short lyrics take a series of animals and objects, and seek their true nature, something that Gerald Manley Hopkins might have called their 'inscape'. These are Rilke's *Dinggedichten* or 'thing poems'. In writing about a panther in a cage seen in Paris' Jardin des Plantes, he is in search of the panther's true experience, trying to express it in its own right, rather than the onlooker's experience. His examination of the palm of a hand (*Handinneres*) explores the idea of 'being' a hand, seeing it as the sole of a foot that no longer walks, and suggesting that the lines of the hand mirror the movements of the stars (as in palmistry). Rilke often returns to the image of the hand, and of touching: the opening poem in the early *Das Stunden-Buch* (*Book of Hours*) declares 'ich fühle: ich kann' ('I feel: I can'), and in his essay on Rodin, he calls the sculptor's work, in a telling phrase, 'die Sprache der Hände' ('the language of the hands'). This is thus part of a continuing debate about poetic language, but the image of the poet staring at the palm of his hand surely also echoes that of Narcissus looking at his reflection, and links clearly to Rilke's 'Spiegel' sonnet.

Like Valéry's, Rilke's work often appears conventional in using familiar verse forms. Indeed, his earlier poems are both beautiful and approachable (even the German is relatively straightforward) in a way that belies assumptions that Modernist equals difficult. This may be a testimony to the extent to which Rilke, like Yeats, has been much imitated, so that acquaintance with later writers, both

English and German, has prepared us for his work. He has also been frequently translated into English. His early *Das Stunden-Buch* was written following a visit to Russia and was intended to appear to have been written by an Orthodox monk, but there remains an element of prayer in much of Rilke's work, so that the sudden outbreak of his late work is perhaps less surprising than it may seem.

The later *Sonnette an Orpheus* are more challenging, and the *Duineser Elegien* are very difficult indeed, both in German and English, both as language and as thought. The sonnets at least seem to build on the earlier work: it is the interconnectedness of ideas and images that develops during the sequence that takes them to a different level of difficulty. But from the overflowing opening line of the first elegy, 'Wer, wenn ich shriee, hörte mich denn aus der Engel Ordnungen' (Who, were I to cry out, would hear me from the ranks of angels') the reader realises that they are faced with a poem that is genuinely an appeal, and one which will demand their undivided attention.

The Poem Itself (150 European poems translated and analysed, ed. Stanley Burnshaw (Penguin 1964) includes most of the first elegy, and is a good place to start.

Although they are very different works, it is impossible not to be conscious that, in the *Duineser Elegien* and the *Four Quartets*, Rilke and Eliot are attempting long philosophical poems, something that will move beyond the lyric. One might indeed suggest that the search for the long poem is one of the elements of Modernism.

Explorations of the self

In Joyce's fiction, there is much that is traditional. For example, his *Portrait of the Artist as a Young Man* is the kind of autobiography in disguise that a 19th-century novelist would feel at ease with, while *Ulysses* (see below, page 35) takes the same young man and follows him further into adult life. Joyce, however, pushes his 19th-century literary inheritance to lengths that Dickens and George Eliot could never have contemplated. His creation of psychological realism takes us into the private thoughts of one character and into the erotic fantasies of another. While other novelists had stated a character's thoughts in the same language as their dialogue – as if there were no difference between someone's outer behavioural life and their inner thought processes – Joyce sets out to dramatise these thoughts and all the public/private psychological discrepancies which they entailed. As a result, his fiction contains prose in which sentences, paragraphs and logical causality break down. And even though Joyce begins his novel, according to 19th-century convention, in his protagonist's infancy, the early pages of *Portrait of the Artist as a Young Man* take the naïve charm of Dickens' opening to *Great Expectations* and push it further into a more abstract depiction of an infant's perceptions. Unlike Dickens, Joyce makes the language he uses mimic the linguistic development of the child in question:

> *My father's family name being Pirrip, and my Christian name being Philip, my infant tongue could make of both names nothing longer or more explicit than Pip. So I called myself Pip and came to be called Pip... As I never saw my father or my mother, and never saw any likeness of either of them (for their days were long before the days of photographs), my first fancies regarding what they were like were unreasonably derived from their tombstones. The shape of the letters on my father's, gave me an odd idea that he was as square, stout, dark man, with curly black hair. From the character and turn of the inscription 'Also Georgiana Wife of the Above,' I drew a childish conclusion that my mother was freckled and sickly.*

> *Once upon a time and a very good time it was there was a moocow coming down along the road and this moocow that was coming down along the road meet a nicens little boy named baby tuckoo...*

As we have seen, Joyce took the rules about *how* a narrator works to unprecedented lengths, as well as a reader's notion of *what* the material of a realistic novel should be.

D. H. Lawrence also took the subject matter of the novel into new areas, so much so that he was prosecuted and his work was banned on more than one occasion. In his stories, he dealt with the theme of childhood, growing up, love and courtship in much the same way that 200 years of novels had done previously, but he focused on sexual attraction and physical intimacy in a far more radical and explicit way than previous writers had attempted. This approach was not, however, gratuitous: Lawrence attributed an almost religious importance to sexuality so that he set out to describe sexual actions and sensations with an attention to detail that shocked many readers. Nor did he limit himself to heterosexuality, examining the homosexual feelings that both men and women experience.

Homosexuality as such never became his central subject: that was left to writers such as E. M. Forster in *Maurice* and Radcliffe Hall in *The Well of Loneliness*, novels that are entirely traditional in their narrative and characterisation, being modern only in their subject matter.

Marcel Proust's work has Romantic sensibilities in its Dickensian exploration of childhood and Balzacian portrait of high-society foibles. Proust however takes that exploration into an examination of adolescence and shows erotically charged flirtations between growing children beyond anything analogous to that between Pip and Estella in *Great Expectations*. In adult life, he presents homosexuality as a fact of family and social life in a way that none of his 19th-century forebears would have considered. In addition, the obsessive detailing of his recollections is not of the same ilk as Balzac's detail of description. While Balzac has a kind of scientific conviction underlying his purposes, Proust's use of detail is not social but personal, its concerns not external but internal.

Musil pushes the limits of the traditional novel in the slowness of the development of his narratives and the ability to examine his narrative from vantage points both far away and close to. He opens *Der Mann ohne Eigenschaften (Man without Qualities)* by describing the weather front affecting the continent, but proceeds through the bureaucratic minutiae of the debates of a committee to celebrate the 70th anniversary of the emperor's accession to the throne of Austria-Hungary. This is an anniversary which the reader knows will never be celebrated because they are afforded the privileged and ironic position of knowing, as the characters cannot, that the First World War is looming, which was to end with the ruling house's abdication.

The comedy is furthered by the country only ever being referred to as Kakania, a coinage based on the German children's word for excrement.

Among his other works, there is a novel about homosexuality and sadism in a boys' school.

Another Modernist author to depict the intricacies of bureaucracy was the Czech novelist and short story writer, **Franz Kafka** (1833–1924). Often seen as an Expressionist due to the nightmarish quality of his intensely felt prose, Kafka was an early Modernist in several important respects. His short story *Die Verwandlung* (*The Metamorphosis*) opens with its haplessly overworked protagonist, Gregor Samsa, waking up to find himself transformed into a giant beetle. By developing this fantastical scenario within largely realist conventions, and providing no frame of reference to interpret the juxtaposition, Kafka is making a statement of Modernist intent, challenging the relationship between the text and the hitherto complacent reader. Moreover, the story's debt to the fairytale genre and absurdist subversion of conventional science echo Yeats' disillusionment with the limits of empirical knowledge, and search for more primitive forms.

Kafka's most epic work, *Das Schloss* (*The Castle*), presents a mysterious anti-hero known only as K embarking on an often contradictory quest, the ultimate purpose of which is never specified. Despite the clearly unreal nature of his narratives, Kafka sticks to the everyday in some ways, indeed he can be seen mocking the bourgeois fussiness and pretensions of his protagonists, for example the clerk Joseph K in *Der Prozess* (*The Trial*). Beckett achieves something similar in some of his fiction, such as *Molloy* (page 50).

By stripping his lead character of any background story, obvious motivations and even a full name, Kafka eschews traditional characterisation and expresses the Modernist concern for the unknowability of the self. For him, the intricate and oppressive bureaucracy in which his characters find themselves caught up is thus an image of modern life, certainly, but also a statement of the truth about the nature of identity and life itself.

This tendency to present characters as pared-down pawns, not as individuals with specified ambitions and coherent psychology, can also be seen in German Expressionist drama of the period. The leading exponent of this movement, **Georg Kaiser** (1878–1945), employed archetypes, defined only in terms of their social function, in a way not dissimilar to Schnitzler's characterisation in *La Ronde*. In addition, Kaiser frequently used the Modernist motif of Dionysian upheaval in his plays, as his characters violently reinvent themselves and make decisive, sometimes erotically-charged breaks with their pasts. This can be seen most clearly in the character of the cashier in perhaps his best-known play *Von Morgen bis Mitternachts* (*From Morning to Midnight*). This man, who in his overworked inhumanity bears a distinct resemblence to Gregor Samsa, steals a large sum from his employer and sets out on a pleasure-seeking mission at breakneck speed. The idea of rupture thus functions both on the level of form and of content, as Expressionist characters enact in their lives what their creators were attempting in their art.

This motif of reinvention is also present in Kafka's unfinished novel *Amerika* (also known as *Der Verschollene*, *The Missing Person*), which shows an exiled European boy leaving the Old World for the New. Although more traditional in its psychological portrayal and narrative technique than his other two full-length novels, *Amerika* is remarkably modern in its presentation of the urban environment. The images evoked by its keenly observed descriptions, whether of machinery on the factory floor or the congested urban landscape, echo the stylised, dehumanised paintings of the Imagists.

T.S. Eliot

T.S Eliot was born to a prosperous American family. A successful student, like Pound, he had the option of pursuing an academic career, and did write a doctoral thesis on philosophy, but ultimately chose to dedicate himself to writing. While writing poetry, he also built up a reputation as a critic. Later in life, he wrote plays, always in verse, which enjoyed differing degrees of success and are occasionally revived. However, it is as a lyric and narrative poet that he is best known. As we shall see, however, 'lyric' and 'narrative' are problematic terms to apply to Eliot's work.

Eliot's work appeared to be something wholly new to the English-speaking world, but he himself pointed to French poetry as a source, citing Laforgue along with late Elizabethan drama as key influences when he began to write in 1908.

Quoted in *The Invisible poet: T. S. Eliot*, Hugh Kenner (W. H. Allen) 1965.

In brief, where English poetry had undergone a dramatic upheaval at the beginning of the 19th century with Romanticism, and then increasingly lost direction and purpose, French Romanticism had begun a little later and had developed into something that resembled Modernism in an organic, unfaltering way. The journey from Hugo through Gautier, Baudelaire, Verlaine and Rimbaud to Mallarmé and on into the 20th century seems continuous and progressive in its aesthetic development.

The significance of late 19th-century French poets to the Anglophone world was quite different to that they had at home. Indeed, Laforgue has tended to be read more carefully and with greater respect abroad than in France itself.

The equivalent is the importance of Edgar Allan Poe in France a century earlier; Baudelaire said he had learned English in order to read Poe.

The Waste Land

Eliot's poem *The Waste Land* (1922) consists of five named sections ('The Burial of the Dead', 'A Game of Chess', 'The Fire Sermon', 'Death by Water' and 'What the Thunder Said'). Each of these sections is further divided into various 'narrative' fragments of varying length.

The Waste Land offers a unified narrative on one level, but on another it presents a series of interlocking and overlapping stories. No one could describe it, however, as narrative in quite the same sense that a novel by Eliot's contemporary D. H. Lawrence is a narrative. There is not a series of causes linked to a series of effects nor a cast of characters that the reader gets to know, linked to one another by a set of recognisable relationships.

This disruption of narrative to the point that we can't keep track of a story is something we might expect from a Modernist work. The poem is in part about sexuality; 'A Game of Chess' contains the account of a woman reporting that she bought some medicine to take (illegally at that time) to terminate a pregnancy. Another section in 'The Fire Sermon' shows a rather clinical seduction raising the topic of sexuality of a particularly inglorious, sordid nature. Another Modernist feature is that the poem narrates the anonymity of city life. 'The Burial of the Dead' shows crowds going by, in which no one looks anyone else in the eye, presenting the city as lonely, rather than convivial. Yet there are no contrasting references to rural life. There is talk of sterility and desert, but no escape into an imagined pastoral utopia or some image of fecundity.

There are distinct characters, certainly, but they appear and disappear spectrally. Are all the women in the poem the same woman merely in different guises and at different moments in her life, or in different moods? This reading would be reinforced by the metamorphic gender of the poem's unifying presence, the prophet Tiresias, who lived as both man and woman according to ancient Greek mythology. It is impossible to ascribe a coherent voice to the work but we can read it as a poem in which the various voices of modern London speak together in cacophony.

It is an interesting exercise to go through *The Waste Land* and try to draw up a list of the cast of characters and voices that appear. It is not an easy task, since it is not always clear which voice implies the presence of which person, nor is it intended to be. Some critics emphasise that Eliot's own married life was difficult at this time, with his wife eventually being committed to what we would now call a mental hospital. This approach tends to read much of what is going on in the 'A Game of Chess' section as a kind of dramatisation of a relationship between husband and wife, and lines such as 'my nerves are bad', and the various recollections of a happier past, are the most immediate elements of the troubled domestic dialogue that might be attempting to convey the neuralgia of Eliot's wife, Vivien. This is certainly a valuable way to read the poem, but it is unlikely to convince many readers that it sums up the 'plot' or adequately recognises all that the poem has to offer. After all, had Eliot wanted to write a kind of one-act *Who's Afraid of Virginia Woolf?*, he could have done so.

The reason he did not write a play or short novel about the breakdown of a marriage was because his subject in *The Waste Land* is much wider than this. For one thing, he is showing that an individual life's breakdown is only one part of a general social malaise. This is done partly by showing the voices of different people from varying social classes. You should be able to recognise aristocratic, upper middle, lower middle and working class voices speaking, even though the class system has changed a good deal since the poem was written. His insistence that something is wrong with society at large also comes through in the quotations from Shakespeare's *Tempest* and the allusions to the Parzival (or grail) story. The 'role' played by history in the poem's story is also a means of saying that it is not merely a personal tragedy that is being written about, but society itself has lost or destroyed something important.

As well as its pertinent social observations, there is also a sense of something sacred underlying the mundane. There is a feeling that in taking part in ordinary life we are also unknowingly taking part in a religious act or rite as the fragments of Christian and Buddhist theology testify.

In his *Autobiographies* Yeats quotes Mallarmé's observation that the age expected a new sacred book to be written. For another modern work that invokes an unfamiliar and unfathomable religious ritual, see the comments on the *Rite of Spring* in Chapter 3.

Eliot's pen also points to an underlying interest in primitive vegetation ceremonies (he takes the title from an early anthropological study in this area), something that again recalls *The Rite of Spring*. Compare the opening of *The Waste Land* with that of the *Canterbury Tales*:

> *Whan that Aprill with his shoures soote*
> *The droghte of March hath perced to the roote*
> *And bathed every venyne in swich licour*
> *Of which vertu engendered is the flour…*

Chaucer is writing a comedy in which natural fruitfulness is expressed in wonderfully smooth and confident verse. Eliot's spring is a painful awakening ('April is the cruellest month') from the safety of winter ('stirring/ Dull roots with spring rain'), an edginess illustrated by the string of awkwardly positioned present participles: 'breeding', 'mixing', 'stirring', 'covering', 'feeding'. These prevent the lines stopping where they want to — with those five commas — forcing on them the evidently unwanted, frustrated energy of enjambement. No wonder 'Spring surprised us'.

In addition to the five sections mentioned earlier, there is something which some might describe as its sixth section, for the poem is followed by a set of notes or glosses written by the author himself. We have already looked at the allusion to Chaucer, but the poem makes frequent use of quotations and calculated misquotations from a range of authors, including Renaissance English dramatists and Romantic French poets, and the notes indicate where many of the citations are from. So are these notes part of the poem itself, and if not, what are they doing there? The short answer is that when it was first submitted, the poem was too short to be published, and the author was asked to provide something to fill the otherwise blank pages. According to this version of events, the notes are of no importance (except to pedants who love chasing down abstruse source material, and academics who have to do this sort of thing for a living). The longer answer is that Eliot, like Pound, Yeats and several others, wanted to remake the public's reading habits and reshape our sense of what tradition entails. Pound, with characteristic bluntness and humour, explains in the middle of his *The Cantos* (which effectively embrace their notes rather than leave them to a separate section):

> I shall have to learn a little greek to keep up with this
> But so will you, drratt you.
>
> *The Cantos* 105.

This is all part of what I earlier called a 'process of devaluing and revaluing of tradition'. In chapter 5 we shall see the way in which Picasso sets out to copy and recreate a series of paintings from art history, remaking them in his own style (or styles).

Ulysses

Joyce also invokes ritual, although to very different effect. *Ulysses* opens with a parody of the mass and contains a number of references to Classical Greek gods. In this, and Joyce's other works, there are a good number of scenes in which Roman Catholic rituals feature directly or are mocked implicitly.

Similarly, both *Ulysses* and *The Waste Land* make frequent reference to earlier works of literature, most notably Homer's *The Odyssey*, but put these references to different literary effect. Homer's ancient Greek epic provides the overall structure of *Ulysses*, and incidents in the story of the Greek hero's journey home from the Trojan War are paralleled chapter by chapter in the story of the mundane yet still extraordinary day in the life of Leopold Bloom in early 19th-century Dublin. But where

> This is the aspect of the book drawn attention to by Eliot in his *'Ulysses*, order and myth' essay.

Eliot is making a series of literary comparisons to darkly tragic, or at least depressing, effect, pointing to the vulgarity, commercialism and loneliness of modern life, Joyce is writing a comic novel. There are endless opportunities to see the ridiculousness of the pomposity and pretention of his characters. While Homer's story shows a loyal wife awaiting a brave husband, fending off suitors, Joyce's shows a singer, Molly Bloom, with a taste for pornography who is having an affair with her agent, and concludes with an extended episode showing her train of thoughts which include a series of sexual fantasies.

Joyce shows us the intricacies of Bloom's point of view, so that we feel closer to him than it had been possible to feel to any previous character in literature. We see him eat, sleep, drink, have a bowel movement and try to stare up the dress of a girl on the beach, while at the same time knowing what the thought processes accompanying these activities are. We also see into the other characters, so that we learn that the girl on the beach is trying to arrange her clothes to expose herself more effectively to Bloom. While he is sexually aroused by the experience, she is telling herself a romantic story about her own imagined life based on the kind of fantasy literature of passionate heroes and adoring heroines that still sells remarkably well today. This is why the novelist George Orwell admired the way that Joyce had discovered 'an America that was under everybody's nose' in showing the inner life of his characters (*Inside the Whale*, 1940). Furthermore, the critic Hugh Kenner has shown the way that Joyce varies the style in which he writes according to the character about whom he is writing, so that his style is modelled on theirs. Gertie MacDonald's, the girl on the beach, literary knowledge of romance and sexual relationships is limited to soppy novels, so her thoughts are written hilariously in the style of these. Joyce is showing that the way we read conditions the way in which we think.

5
Modernism in the visual arts

Modernist painters did not begin life as Modernists. Most started off painting in a 19th-century style, assuming the academic realist values of a now devalued Romantic movement. However different their origins and their works, Modernist painters all came to discover that the visual language they had been taught was inadequate to represent the world they observed. They knew that if they painted in the style of their artistic forefathers, the results would inevitably be false.

> Compare this with how Modernist writers described the limitations of the forms and techniques they inherited (see page 29).

Picasso

Picasso's father, a provincial Spanish art teacher, was so stunned by his son's prodigal brilliance that, when the boy was 14, he gave him his own palette and brushes and swore never to paint again. He set the young Picasso various subjects

> John Berger considers the significance of this anecdote in *The Success and Failure of Picasso*, Vintage 1998.

to paint, taken from the repertoire of conventional 19th-century painting, and the very conventionality of these exercises must have made them easy for the gifted child to master. But his early success left Picasso with a lifelong yearning to discover both the actual boundaries of his talent and what he deemed the real nature of art. This enquiry led Picasso to develop an interest in 'primitive' art, especially the African masks of which he built up a significant collection.

> Compare this with the recourse Stravinsky had to primitive religion in his music.

Picasso moved from Spain to Paris, the centre of the art world, and came under the influence both of the Pre-Raphaelite Burne-Jones and of various contemporary styles (including Impressionism, Post-impressionism and Symbolism). He depicted poverty, but not in the academic style that his father might have expected. His 'Blue Period' paintings show poor people who inhabit a world that is not quite recognisable. It is not that the individuals are distorted or that their environment is dreamlike, just that the implicit feeling of the painting is elusive, whereas a strictly academic painting of poverty would have created a very clear feeling of pity, whimsy, or horror. Picasso leaves viewers not quite sure of the significance of what they are looking at.

The anthropological materials which imperialism had introduced to the arts arena and curious market contributed to his thinking on the role of **mimesis** in painting, an issue that the advent of photography had raised. Where Klimt had painted in a manner that merged realism, in his depiction of hands and faces, with the unreality of abstract pattern (as if the subjects' clothes, material surroundings and wallpaper had all been placed in the same plane as the living person), Picasso sought to integrate distortion and shock into his works, using the African art of his private collection as an influence. Thus he moves from the rough treatment of poverty in *The Frugal Meal* (1904), which is closely related to Van Gogh's *Potato Eaters* (1885), to the *Family of Saltimbanques* (1905), a slightly strange descendent of Watteau's playful world, to *Les Demoiselles d'Avignon* (1906/1907), which is to the history of art what *Ulysses* and the *Rite of Spring* are to literature and music respectively. Picasso's progress here looks like a journey of staggering speed, but in fact these are all clearly defined stages, not least because the sketches that Picasso made when preparing the *Demoiselles* have survived.

Les Demoiselles d'Avignon

This painting shows a group of thin, awkward-looking young women. Their poses are both artistic and gratuitously suggestive, since their raised, flexed arms, the positioning of their hands behind their heads, the provocative lifting of their breasts, is in keeping with the painting's subject, that of a group of prostitutes in a brothel. This topic, and the way some of the women stare challengingly at the viewer, clearly relate to **Manet**'s *Olympia* (1865), a portrait of a self-possessed, recumbent, naked prostitute staring confidently out of the picture. Here is a painting that clearly challenges the prevailing bourgeois assumptions about how women in general and prostitutes in particular should view themselves. Olympia is neither modest nor ashamed, she is not flirting and smiling; she is asserting herself as a part of the society that supports her existence.

Because of the rise to intellectual dominance of Marxist cultural analyses in the mid-20th-century, the word 'bourgeois' has been overused. It is simply a French word for the urban middle classes and by extension their value code.

The preparatory sketches show how Picasso experimented by converting, in one case, what was originally a relatively conventional study of a woman's head by stages into both a geometrical study and a distortion. The planes and lines that together make up the woman's face are emphasised, and the individuality of its own specific curves are eliminated. At the same time, Picasso finds that this process brings the image more closely into line with the way faces are treated in the iconography of traditional African masks, as the individual elements of the face are emphasised at the expense of the composition – the whole face itself.

The privileging of the total composition, or an overall 'likeness', over depicting the individual elements had in general terms been a mark of the Renaissance and all the art that stemmed from it. Picasso is thus in part overturning four hundred years of artistic practice.

In the sketches for the posing of the models, Picasso also simplifies, geometrises and ritualises the figures. Rather than concealing the underlying structure of the painting, he makes it obvious by using the contrasting pink-browns and blue-grey-whites to divide the picture into three clear vertical zones: in effect, the left-hand woman, the two central directly-faced women, and the two figures on the right. Consider the way the faces are treated differently according to the zone in which they are found. Picasso also dispenses with the traditional use of fore-, mid- and background; women, table, fruit, draperies and all other objects are placed in the same plane. This process is again not unlike something that can be observed in Klimt's work. Klimt created a geometrical and ritual version of reality that promotes something conventional (in both nature and art), such as an individual face or two faces meeting in a kiss, into the profound artistic significance of a Catholic altarpiece or an Orthodox icon. Picasso by contrast brings out the essential savagery and brutality found in the everyday. Just as Joyce and Eliot put modern relationships into a much older context through a recognisable cultural-linguistic appeal to the world of Homer, Dante and Shakespeare, so Picasso is showing the modern world of the brothel as part of a larger continuity with prehistory and with the alien world of African society.

What are the implications of this for how we think about the *Rite of Spring*?

Nevertheless, the composition of the picture and the grouping of the women are strongly reminiscent of the European tradition of the nude. For example, there are several paintings in several styles of *The Judgement of Paris*, in all of which a young man examines a group of three naked women. The ancient Greek story was that the young Trojan prince Paris was asked by three competing goddesses to judge which was the most beautiful. The jealousy and anger that resulted from his decision is one of the root causes of the Trojan war. John Russell has suggested that Picasso used the format of Rubens' version of this subject. Like those in the writings of Joyce and Eliot, this classical allusion leaves open the question of whether modern life suffers by comparison with the grand cultural archetypes of the past. Both Rubens and Picasso are questioning the role and nature of women. Where Rubens concentrates on curves in women's bodies, Picasso emphasises their angularity. I have already pointed to the way in which Picasso renders the faces, but the same can be said of the bodies he depicts: they are not weighted and curved, but hard and full of sharp corners. Rubens was celebrating fertility and corporeality, enjoying flesh and by extension life; Picasso is drawing attention to harshness, to the underlying bones in the body and perhaps, by implication, the underlying poverty and hunger that motivates these women's dealings with men.

John Russell, *The Meanings of Modern Art*, Thames and Hudson 1981.

This is a point that is picked up later in the century by several women artists such as Paula Rego.

The posture of the woman squatting to the front right of the painting is associated with defecation, childbirth and a prostitute washing after a customer has left, and possesses a similar calculated ugliness to the choreography of Nijinsky in the *Rite of Spring* six years later. Yet the final painting renders the face strikingly like a self portrait by Picasso. Moreover, the fact that the right-hand figure in his *Three Dancers* (1925) seems to be a descendant of this figure lends some support to the idea that during the process of composition, this figure changed gender. This would also link up with the fact that in Rubens' *The*

Judgement of Paris there has to be the figure of Paris standing in a position of spectatorship to the female bodies. Surely this figure has metamorphosed in order to cast Picasso in that role, a role that implicitly also makes us realise that an artist painting a nude is thus aligned with prostitutes' customers as a voyeur, a judgement which can be extended to the voyeuristic position of the individual appreciating the work itself. The painting has turned the *Paris* tradition on its head by making our attitudes, not their bodies, the object of the picture's *Judgement*.

There is thus more than what we might call ritual distortion in Picasso's treatment of women. The deliberate emphasis on distortion and the underlying savagery of a prostitute's relationship with men is a theme which can be found in other Picasso paintings. In a painting entitled *Figure*, Picasso reduces the model to an outline which only barely succeeds in retaining the female form, and within which there is the mark of a slit which serves both for her mouth and for her genitals. Do paintings like this contain an implicit note of violence towards their subjects? Does this attitude contain some of the late-Romantic sense of the dangerousness of women and women's sexuality given new Modernist guise?

This is another aspect of late Romanticism that translated from literature to film, which showed an early predisposition to *femmes fatales*, brooding, vampire-like figures inherited from pre-Raphaelite and Symbolist art. There is often a flavour of this in the presentation of Greta Garbo, for example, but also Bette Davies and the female lead in *The Maltese Falcon* who is placed in calculated opposition to Sam Spade's brave, but more conventionally feminine, secretary.

Epstein

As we have already noted, many people were excited and many others were shocked by these artistic developments. We can catch a glimpse of this in Doris Lessing's novel Martha Quest, which is set in 1930s colonial Rhodesia (modern Zimbabwe) and draws on the author's own experiences. Set at a time when finance and diplomacy were first bringing the colony's inhabitants into contact with modern art, the novel shows the offence which many traditionalists took with the implication that these works somehow represented them. The narrator's conventional mother calls Epstein and Havelock Ellis 'disgusting', claiming that if future civilisations discovered such artefacts, they would consider her generation to have been 'savages'.

The unstated occasion of this fictional scenario was probably the historical Rhodesian government's occupation of the British Medical Association's former headquarters in London. The 18 Jacob Epstein figures which had decorated the building were mutilated.

Like Picasso, Epstein drew on African art in his creation of a pointedly earth-bound scheme of imagery. Considering the settlers' reasons for detesting Epstein's work gives us an insight into the values and presuppositions that underpinned imperialism. However, it may also indicate at least a part of the (perhaps antagonistic) motivation behind Epstein's and Picasso's adoption of African models. It certainly is a classic example of the gulf of opinion that opened between artists and those who followed the arts closely on the one hand, and wider public opinion on the other.

Rock Drill

Epstein's most famous works remains *Rock Drill* (1913–1914), which provided the title for a section of Pound's *The Cantos*. Epstein had initially exhibited a plaster human figure set on top of a real pneumatic drill. This robot-like figure, its face concealed by a visor, became as much a symbol of modern life as the railways had been in the Romanticism of Turner and Tolstoy, and electric pylons were later to become in the early verse of Stephen Spender. Epstein indeed considered whether the piece should include a motor to make the piece move (1913 was also the year in which Duchamp's *Bicycle Wheel*, often cited as the first example of kinetic art, was exhibited). The work certainly reflected the interests of its age, and indeed the company Epstein had been keeping, such as his involvement with the Vorticists and Futurists.

Futurism is sometimes said to have its origins in composer Ferruccio Busoni's *Entwurf einer neuen Ästhetik der Tonkunst* (*Sketch of a New Aesthetic of Music*), but its most famous exponent is unquestionably Filippo Tommaso Marinetti, whose 1909 Futurist manifesto defined the style and attitude. Technology, with its provision of speed and implicit violence, acquired an artist credibility it had not had since such Enlightenment painters as Joseph Wright. Industrialisation, and particularly cars and aeroplanes, and the built environment were to take over from Romanticism's landscape as the key sources of artistic inspiration.

So do we experience *Rock Drill* as a celebration of human mastery of the power of technology, drawing on Futurist visual rhetoric, or does it leave the viewer suspicious that the figure is not heroic but menacing? Epstein later removed the drill, reduced the figure from full- to half-length, altered the arms and cast the resulting torso in bronze. The result, first exhibited in 1916, is what is now on show, although reconstructions of the original are also shown, as is an initial charcoal sketch for the piece.

Epstein wrote that the idea for the original construct came out of his pre-war 'ardour for machinery', which was short-lived. His autobiography (1940) describes how he mounted on an actual drill 'a machine-like robot, visored, menacing, and carrying within itself its progeny, protectively ensconced'. The original figure, as the charcoal sketch shows, represents the figure as integrated into the drill: his legs merge into two of the machine's, while the third leg of the tripod is perhaps suggestive of that mechanised eroticism implicit in the sculptor's comment on 'carrying within itself its progeny'. Is the later cut-down version therefore an attempt to neuter the power of the original figure? It is certainly a move towards capturing it in a more conventional sculptural material.

Cubism

As well as being a remarkable painting in its own right, *Les Demoiselles d'Avignon* is credited as marking the origins of a new movement in the visual arts. As John Berger writes: 'By painting *Les Demoiselles d'Avignon*, Picasso provoked Cubism.'

John Berger, *The Success and Failure of Picasso*, Penguin 1965.

Cubism is conventionally seen as having been developed by the partnership of **Georges Braque** and Picasso, beginning in 1908. However, looking at what in any other picture one would call the 'background' and the use of drapery, we can see the wider reach of a Cubist approach. Again, there is a kind of link back to the jewel-like tesserae of Klimt, but Picasso and Braque were quite deliberate in developing Cubism within a drab colour scheme. Cubist paintings are frequently chromatically restrained, with colours chosen from a narrow range of blue, grey and brown palettes. As we shall see later with Jackson Pollock (see page 53), Cubism invites the viewer to participate in the process of painting itself. In the painting of a still life, the painter normally paints or reflects a static arrangement. Braque's and Picasso's still lives actively move the subject around in the painting itself, looking at it from different angles and trying out different positions. The painting itself contains within its borders a series of interlocking planes which regard the subject simultaneously from a number of differing perspectives and vantage points. The viewer may find it difficult at first to see that an abstract painting is in fact the study of a familiar scene. This level of viewing difficulty is, however, necessary to the Cubist project, because the various lines, shades and angles that make up each of the elements in the composition have been to some degree abstracted from the source object and harmonised with those drawn from the other objects. And this concern for design left little time for colour.

From 1912 Braque also experimented with collage, and in reproduction it is impossible sometimes to determine what is collage and what is standard painting. His co-mingling of newsprint and aspects of cafe life are often examined purely as studies in design, with no consideration of subject matter. But in fact these still lives are frequently based around tables, bottles and newspapers, because since the latter part of the 19th century, the cafe had assumed the social centrality of the salon and its predecessor the court. With the aristocratic patron no longer providing financial refuge and creative constraints, artists had the job of selling their own work, but they were also free to please themselves in choices of subject and style. The only comment and criticism which they were concerned with was that of their peer group, the fellow artists they met in the Parisian cafes. These still lives are thus, in the self-reflexive tradition, paintings about the art of painting.

The assumption that the newspaper clippings were chosen at random has also been challenged. Patricia Leighton suggested that there is an implicit political message to the collages. *Re-Ordering the Universe: Picasso and Anarchism, 1897–1914*, Princeton University Press 1989.

Fauvism and Matisse

Henri Matisse (1869–1954) studied under the Symbolist painter Moreau but also absorbed the influence of Gauguin. By 1905, he had acquired followers in the shape of Vlaminck and Rouault, and a reviewer had coined the label 'Les Fauves', or the wild beasts, to collectively describe their body of work. We can probably still understand savagery in the context of Gauguin, or the *Rite of Spring*, for example. But looking back on Matisse, it may be difficult to see what in this supremely calm, meditative painter's work can possibly have seemed so wild and savage. In contrast to Cubism, Matisse used strong, often primary, colours, and used them without obvious regard for mimetic truth. He seemed to be applying bright colours in ignorance of (or brutal contempt for) the world he observed around him. Looking at the famous portrait of fellow *fauve* André Derain (1905, Tate Modern, London), the viewer might say that objectively there simply isn't a green strip around the right hand side of the man's face, nor a purple one on his chin and neck. It might seem to a casual viewer that this use of colour is like that of the German Expressionists, where it was part of a calculated assault on the viewer and his society, along with the shortening of figures and the cartoon-like distortion of faces, distortions which match the harmonic and melodic ones in *Pierrot Lunaire*.

> Reading early Brecht and listening to Weill and Eisler would complement an interest in German Expressionist art.

Matisse set out to create an artistic world of harmony and order as a refuge from, and corrective to, the actual world of war and poverty. As a result, his paintings often have titles that invoke pleasure, dance and music: *Luxe, calme et volupté, Bonheur de vivre, La Musique, La Dance*. Matisse had set colours free from the imprisonment of a plainly descriptive function to a more vividly expressive one. Matisse is perhaps more aware of the temperature of colours than their strict chromatic presence. His *Dessert* (1908) thus has the Whistler-like subtitle 'Harmony in red', although it might be more fittingly titled 'Study in wealth and warmth'.

Where Picasso shocked those expecting smooth curves by offering angularity and awkwardness, Matisse structured his work around circles and ellipses. One of his several *Danse* paintings (Hermitage, St Petersburg) is essentially made up of three colours, a cold blue and green and a hot orange, thus fitting with the 'fauvist' label. In addition, the bodies are distorted, thus forging some link with Expressionism. However, the distortion is clearly in order to show their participation in, or perhaps submission to, the dance. The five figures hold hands in a circle, but careful examination reveals a series of other curved shapes organising the whole. The tension in the work is present in the fact that the circle is in fact broken, as the front centre figure has lost hold of, or not yet clasped, the hand of the figure on the left. It is rewarding to compare this celebratory work with Picasso's various beach scenes in which solid statuesque people relax or play.

> Consider first why John Berger (*Success and Failure of Picasso*) is hostile to this aspect of Picasso's work, and second how Robert Hughes (*Shock of the New* 1980, Thames and Hudson 1991) changed his views concerning Matisse relative to Picasso.

Kandinsky and colour

Like those of Matisse, the titles of **Wassily Kandinsky**'s (1866–1944) paintings – *Improvisations*, *Impressions*, and *Compositions* – often reflect the influence of music. His parents had played the piano and the zither, and he himself had been taught piano and cello as a child. As an adult, although a lecturer in law, he wrote on spirituality, a subject that was of lifelong concern and which influenced his work (in 1911 he published *On the Spiritual in Art*). In 1895 he went to an exhibition of French Impressionist art, which included Monet's *Haystacks at Giverny*.

Living at Argenteuil on the banks of the Seine, **Claude Monet** had been exploring how the supposely known and familiar world is in a continual process of change. Our witness to it in art had to reflect that dynamism: within the static world of the painting, the artist needed to represent both the moment he was painting and the continual flux of which it was a brief extract. Monet painted series of works in the 1890s, showing the way in which a building (the cathedral of Notre Dame in Rouen) or a landscape or object (waterlilies, poplars and indeed haystacks) changed from moment to moment as the light changed during the course of a day.

Kandinsky said later that he had been disturbed that the subject of the painting was not obvious, and he had felt that this was in some way not right. The exhibition clearly had its effect, though, as, aged thirty, he went to Munich to study fine arts. In Germany he drew on Expressionist influences and undertook *fauviste* experiments with colour, associating with the *Blaue Reiter* group, which took its name from a 1913 painting of his.

Despite the unease created by Monet, Kandinsky soon began to experiment with the natural musicality of colour: he described it as causing the colours to 'sing'. As well as referring to singing, Kandinsky called colour the keyboard on which the artist plays, and declared that he saw colour he heard music, much as the composer Messiaen was to do later (see page 51). He was creating an art in which the visual eperience was being liberated from the subject of the painting. Critics sometimes point to the lost subject, but the experience of looking at Kandinsky's paintings is one of involvement in the relationships between the colours, and the movement of the forms.

His involvement with the Bauhaus, the art and architecture school founded by Walter Gropius, contributed to a development away from organic to a more geometrical style (*One White II*, 1923). This is an essentially optimistic art, yet it was condemned by Nazi and Soviet authorities alike, as their definitions of optimism were too narrow to accommodate it. Indeed, Kandinsky's abstract works were included in the infamous *Entartete Kunst* (degenerate art) exhibition, alongside works by Matisse and Picasso, as well as by Beckmann, Chagall, Heckel, Kirchner and Nolde. Under both tyrannies, art was to be representative and heroic. All distortions of the image were associated with mental and physical disability, and were eliminated from galleries at much the same time and for much the same reasons as the disabled were being eliminated from German society.

6
Where did Modernism go?

If Modernism was such a pervasive movement, and affected so many art forms, what happened in the arts after the Modernist movement had spent its revolutionary force?

Diversification

In several cases, individual artists developed different styles and embarked on new projects. Stravinsky began writing in a Neoclassical idiom, exploring the styles of previous eras. He composed *Apollon musagète* (1928), which is very different from the *Rite of Spring* in that the rhythmic and harmonic language used are far closer to a conventional one. Richard Strauss similarly moved from the jagged sound of *Elektra* and *Salomé* to the better tempered *Der Rosenkavalier*. His *Arabella* combines a Wagnerian orchestral sound with a cross-dressing bourgeois comedy of manners, complete with disguises and farcical misunderstandings. Later still, Stravinsky unexpectedly adopted Serialism, a technique he had spent the whole of his previous career actively shunning, and produced a series of post-Webern works. In this way, curiously enough, he fulfilled Debussy's prophecy (or warning) of half a century earlier, that the younger composer showed signs of falling under the dangerous influence of Schoenberg.

> Stravinsky was not happy with the original version of *Apollon musagète* and rewrote it as *Apollo* (1947).

While Picasso too explored the art of previous periods, he seemed quite happy to move from idiosyncratic copies of Ingres or Poussin to Cubism, then Expressionism, and on to ceramics or sculptures made from *objets trouvés*, without feeling the need to take any particular artistic direction to its natural conclusion.

Eliot was received into the Church of England. His later period's greatest achievement is the *Four Quartets*. These poems take the writing style Eliot had developed partly under Pound's tutelage, and which had resulted in *The Waste Land*, but infuse it with the traditional language of Christian mysticism. In a rather lyrical style, Eliot is intent on offering moral resolution, as if he were determined to end each of the four poems in the set with a perfect cadence.

A return to the past

Linked to this increasing diversification is the mid-20th-century counter-revolution against Modernism's upheaval of the arts. A generation of poets, composers and artists grew up to whom the failure of Modernist works of art to appeal to a wide popular audience and readership made it look like a kind of old-school 'art for art's sake', an elitist rewrite of Romanticism. Some of the reactionaries in question deliberately set about writing in forms that the Modernist movement had brushed aside. Now a generation of artists asserted that their rediscovered tonality and mimesis were more modern than Modernism. Eliot was not the name to drop: Auden was .

A political agenda

This rejection of Modernism's elitist excess resulted in part from the increasing popularity of socialism and communism among Europe's intellectual classes. Many assumed that country after country would see Marxist revolutions, and that the job of the artist in every medium was to support this process. Accordingly, poems which no one could recite and tunes which no one could whistle seemed an unjustifiable and decadent luxury.

Where the First World War had looked like a meaningless abomination and the post-war settlement a shallow nightmare, the Russian Revolution, the rise of Fascism, the Depression and the Spanish Civil War created a socio-political agenda that many creative artists felt they had to address directly in their work. The technical term was '**engagé**', or engaged in the sense of getting involved and politically motivated. Modernism was not an approach that readily lent itself to writing political pamphlets or rallying songs, and in an era of mass movements, any artist with political ideals clearly wanted to address a mass audience. Equally, given the heroic status and, to some extent, glamour of creative artists, both fascist and communist movements sought to co-opt artists on to their steering committees. Ezra Pound lent his support to Mussolini's Italian Fascist party and Bertold Brecht to the German Communist Party, though neither ever officially joined.

Shostakovich began composing in an era of excited experimentation, when some artists believed that the Russian Revolution was attempting in politics something analogous to what Modernism was attempting in art. As things turned out, Russia (the USSR) was seized by Stalin, whose tastes differed little from those of Hitler. Both leaders wanted to constrain the arts to an essentially low-grade, 19th-century agenda, emphasising the heroic and the sentimental. It is interesting to note that in both Nazi Germany and Soviet Russia, jazz was banned by the state. When he attempted to depart from this official agenda, Shostakovich was heavily criticised.

Shostakovich only actually joined the Communist Party after the death of Stalin in 1960 (a sign of his ability to distinguish communist ideals from Stalin's perversion of them). Webern by contrast was a card-carrying member of the Nazi party, as were conductor Von Karajan and soprano Elizabeth Schwartzkopf.

While Brecht's œuvre may have evolved from the Expressionism of his earliest plays to something more like politically-conscious Naturalism in his later works, he retained Modernist sympathies in his commitment to stirring audiences' cultural sensibilities. His *Verfremdungseffekt*, known in English as 'alienation technique', was designed to direct audiences towards the Marxist ideology underlying his plays, but its aesthetic is still Modernist. Moreover, the way in which Brecht prioritises social class over personal foibles in his characterisation provides echoes of *La Ronde*, the transitional referenced in the Preface (page 5).

Picasso, faced with the abdication of the monarchy in his native Spain, and an uprising by much of the army against the elected Republican government, decided to remain in France. The

> Unlike Brecht, Picasso did actually join the Communist Party – of France, his adopted home.

civil war resulted in a famous massacre in the historic Basque city of *Guernica*. In response to this, Picasso painted a very famous work which is strikingly successful in drawing on the vocabulary of Modernism. The distortion of faces, the breakdown in the human figure, the extremes sought by Expressionism: all of this is put to powerful effect in *Guernica*'s depiction of armed violence and mass murder. Picasso's later attempt to repeat the success of *Guernica*, this time in response to reports of war crimes during the Korean War, produced a far feebler work in which a group of science-fiction soldiers carry out a mass execution armed with what look like toys. Comparisons between this later work and Edouard Manet's *Execution of Maximilian* (c.1867/8) are illuminating.

Some would assert that Modernism did not die out but rather reinvented itself. A movement emerged that resembled Modernism but is probably better understood as '**mechanised Romanticism**'. This took the language of Romanticism, with its emphasis on heroic achievement and the determination to make an imposing statement, but transposed it from the 19th century's natural world, in which the sublime was the natural expression of the heroic, to the realm of the machine and the city. Like Marinetti's cars, the seemingly endless Soviet cantatas on the subject of new state-directed industrial achievements bear a similar relationship to industry as Shelley or Schumann did to the natural world.

Postmodernism is another cultural movement which defines itself in terms of Modernism's cultural inheritance, although this relationship is often a subversive, antagonistic one. Postmodernist artists do not sidestep Modernism, indeed they use many of its approaches, but with an emphasis on playfulness and self-reflexivity. This new sense of artistic irreverence has infuriated straight-laced Modernist disciples almost as much as the *Rite* once infuriated traditionalists.

Lichtenstein's and **Warhol**'s use of commercial art offended Modernists and traditionalists alike. Their work was modern in its tendency to use unfamiliar materials such as plastic, plywood and aluminium, rather than bronze and marble, while their referencing of cartoons and advertisements is also reminiscent of the snatches of street music in Charles Ives (not to mention Schoenberg: see page 17), and of the pub scene in *The Waste Land*.

> The tendency of some modern painters to use cheap and commercial paints rather than oil paints has created a major problem for conservers since house paint and car paint were never intended to last very long. A number of masterpieces, from Van Gogh to Jackson Pollock, are deteriorating rapidly.

From Godot to the kitchen sink

Modernism was, to some extent, able to renew itself. Eliot's poetry of voices suggests that he could have become a great verse dramatist, and beginning with his *Sweeney Agonistes*, he did attempt plays. Although these did enjoy some commercial success they became progressively less adventurous. In fact, the Modernist dramatic potential in his work lay dormant until it was picked up by a disciple not of his but of Joyce, **Samuel Beckett**. Beginning with *Waiting for Godot* (1955), Beckett's plays enraged unprepared audiences, convinced that they were at best a Rorschach Test and at worst a confidence trick, just as Arnold Bennett had once asked Eliot whether the notes to *The Waste Land* were a joke. In Beckett we see the horror of life's meaninglessness, the collapse of civilisation, the dispassionate nature of failing marriages and the constant determination of men and women to live lives of self-delusion. These are all familiar Modernist paradigms, but the work reads like a Naturalist tragedy rewritten as a Modernist comedy.

> Arnold Bennett is the successful man of letters parodied in Pound's *Hugh Selwyn Mauberly*, 'Mr Nixon'.

After years of neglect, and even with the beginnings of critical success, Beckett's status took time to be established. At the time of *Godot*'s first production, audiences and readers were so attuned to the mid-20th-century dominance of political art, especially literature drawing attention to class conflict, that the real theatrical event seemed to take place the following year in the shape of **John Osborne's** *Look Back in Anger*. Half a century later, Beckett's play seems as challengingly new as ever; Osborne's play which announced, despite CND campaigns, the dishonest invasion of Suez and the crushing of the Hungarian uprising, that there were no great causes left, already seems as out of date as a dance tune on an EP or a newspaper from that era. Adorno, who had attacked Stravinsky, took to Beckett's work and appreciated his plays' successful fusion of low art (music hall influences) with the high art of Modernism; having absorbed their influence, he revised his opinion of Stravinsky to some extent. Adorno ('Trying to Understand Endgame') noted the power with which Beckett adopted the subject of meaninglessness. The well-documented links to Joyce should not blind us to Beckett also being Mallarmé's disciple, especially in his responding to creative sterility by adopting that sterility as a subject in itself and seeing in it a pertinent truth about the human condition. Beckett's sense of menace and comedy is also reminiscent of the novels of **Franz Kafka** (see page 31), although the comedy in Kafka's writings has been largely ignored by critics and translators alike.

> In France, the play's director was told *En Attendant Godot* would never succeed since it did not contain a homosexual, a woman or a communist. That comment sums up neatly mid-20th-century expectations of drama.

Beckett's fiction

A young Irish writer, Beckett not surprisingly was a great admirer of Joyce. He became a family friend (even being seen as a possible husband for Joyce's daughter Lucia at one stage) and assisted him in the early stages of the composition of *Finnegan's Wake* in a secretarial role. As a result, Beckett's early work suffered from what American critic Harold Bloom might term an 'anxiety of influence' in that the young writer struggled to assimilate the older writer's influence without being completely taken over by it. Joyce's writing valued a conscious display of knowledge through the use of allusion, layering the everyday over a mythic structure, and taking a delight in the complexities of language. In trying to replicate these Modernist features, Beckett's early prose often appeared stilted and self-consciously learned, most notably in *Dream of Fair to Middling Women* and *More Pricks than Kicks* (even the titles are literary jokes in both cases, the former parodying Chaucer the latter the New Testament). In order to subvert Joyce's seminal Modernist work Ulysses, Beckett chose to move away from the bold experimentations in language and form of the kind that typified Joyce's work by exhibiting 'a mocking attitude to words, through words'. In a comparison of his works with those of his former employer, Beckett talks in terms of adding and subtracting, contrasting his 'impoverishment' of language with the constant linguistic expansionism to which Joyce's drafts bear witness.

In *Beckett Remembering, Beckett Remembered*, ed. James Knowlson, Bloomsbury 2006.

Beckett chose to remain in France following the German invasion in 1940, when as an Irish national he could have left. He also at this time shifted over to writing in French in preference to English as a way (says James Knowlson in the biography whose title is itself a quote from Beckett, *Damned to Fame*) of escaping the influence of Joyce.

In Beckett's *The Unnameable*, the third of three prose works collectively titled *Trilogy*, this concept of subtraction reaches its fullest realisation. In Joyce's *Ulysses*, Leopold Bloom's mind seems to be perfectly transcribed and contained within the language of exhaustively detailed streams of consciousness. *The Unnameable* expresses the inadequacy of language to narrate a unified sense of selfhood:

> 'Where now? Who now? When now? Unquestioning. I, say I.
> Unbelieving.'

Indeed, while Joyce's Leopold and Molly Bloom are highly sensory, corporeal creations, the voice of *The Unnameable* appears to be a disembodied voice. *Ulysses* revels in its ability to narrate the finest details of the mind's thought patterns; Beckett's novel views the idea of expressing an independent subjectivity as a fallacy. The unnamed narrator of the novel appears more of a hollowed out vessel than an individual consciousness, allowing the free-flow of voices to spew forth from its ventriloquised mouth: 'from my sleeping mouth the lies would pour, about me.' (*The Unnameable*, page 312).

Joyce's style expressed a sense of the wealth of language and the richness of human lives. Beckett's communicates exhaustion and pointlessness: even in those novels that contain action, the actions of characters are often circular and his narratives are full of descriptions of crawling and walking with crutches. Beckett was the writer who discovered the inherent humour as well as despair within entropy, a topic that became fashionable in later American fiction. Beckett's characters often tell lies about themselves (in his play *Not I* denial is perhaps the central purpose of the speaker's flood of words) and at the end of the first novel in the Trilogy, *Molloy*, the narrator of the second half of the book deliberately denies the truth of the beginning of his own narrative. The narrator of the first half confesses early on that he no longer knows how to work. The dying narrator of the second novel *Malone Dies* attempts to tell stories but interrupts himself with comments on his own narration such as 'what tedium… no, that won't do… this is awful'.

Lawrence's legacy

The examination of social class inherent in the literature of this period drew heavily on the work of writers like D. H. Lawrence, and there was practically a school of novelists and playwrights who wrote of working class life in the industrial north of England. Out of this, a number of successful films, some of which had started as plays emerged, such as *A Taste of Honey* and television series, including the seemingly indefatigable *Coronation Street* (1960s–present day).

But these so-called angry young men had only adopted the class issues in Lawrence's work. They entirely missed his metaphysics, which is perhaps more striking in his poetry (some of which had appeared, odd though it may sound now, in *Georgian Poetry*). In the work of **Ted Hughes** (1930–1998), Lawrence's attention to the detail of plants and

> Lawrence is not the only influence: Hughes' 'Thought-fox' has been compared to Rilke's 'Der Panther', and also owes something to Rilke's 'Dinggedichten'.

animals was developed. Hughes' first admirers were excited by the prospect of a new nature poet, but in *Crow*, he brought those themes together with something altogether more reminiscent of Eliot, with a cityscape and a sense of the potential for violence in both people and animals. Similarly, the marriage element in *The Waste Land* leads to the 'confessional school', to the poetry of Roethke, Lowell, Sexton and Plath, among others.

The exploration of sexuality in Lawrence's fiction was picked up by several writers. In *Lolita*'s description of the sexual relationship of a middle-aged man and his teenage step daughter, some critics decided that **Vladimir Nabokov** (1899–1977) had written a new *Lady Chatterley's Lover*. The comparison is not without value, but it does fail to reckon with Lawrence's Modernist passion and Nabokov's Postmodernist humour. Nabokov is assuredly not trying to promote an appreciation of paedophile relationships, but he is teaching us to look again at the literature of courtship and seduction which he is parodying, as well as the human capacity for self-deception and delusion. In this respect, he picks up on the Modernist issues of narrative uncertainty and readerly trust.

At the end of the 19th century, some painters had created a modern version of the late-Romantic style, a movement sometimes called 'Edwardian art' in

England. Tissot, Frith, Solomon and others painted pictures in which there was an implicit 'story', reflecting the cultural dominance of the novel, just as the rise to prominence of programme music had done in the Romantic era. In a typical work from this movement, an upper-middle-class couple arrive too early for a ball, a lower-middle-class couple stare nervously at the menu while the waiter smirks: these are small instances of a social life that the viewer is supposed to recognise and feel at home with.

> It is rewarding to consider how this approach is so different from what Edouard Manet (1832–1883) was doing in his own 'realistic' depictions of the *Bar at the Folies Bergères*.

Many mid-20th-century artists such as **Edward Hopper** (1882–1967) did something similar, although they tended to concentrate on the lower classes, and to eschew 'charm'. **Ben Shahn's** figures (1898–1969) can have a heroic quality about them, rather like the characters in John Steinbeck's *The Grapes of Wrath* (1939). The spirit evoked is very much that of the heroism of labour, or physical effort, a spirit abundantly clear in Soviet art. These painters were influenced by the aesthetics of cinema, with its manipulation of lighting and camera angles. Indeed, *Nighthawks*, by Hopper, might almost be a scene from a film starring Humphrey Bogart due to its emphasis on the emptiness of the street and the bar and, by extension, the hollowness of the lives of the people depicted.

> This painting in turn became a model for a set in the Hollywood version of *Pennies from Heaven*.

I have already observed how Beckett's plays are a challenging combination of the erudite playfulness of Joyce and the fragmentary abstraction of Eliot's work, creating an entirely unique aesthetic. Similarly, **Olivier Messiaen** (1908–1992) was open about his admiration for both Debussy and the *Rite of Spring*. His influences included Indian music and birdsong, which he adored and transcribed. All these influences come together to create highly innovative music. His *Turanglîla-symphony* fascinated and mystified its first reviewers. The music swells and sinks back rather like film music, and some listeners objected to what they deemed the 'tackiness' of some of the melodic effects. In contrast to the luxuriance of this 70-minute symphony, Messiaen is also famous for his *Quatuor pour le fin du temps* (Quartet for

> *Messiaen: Quatuor pour la fin du temps*, Anthony Pople and Julian Rushton, CUP.

the end of time, 1941). Written while he was a prisoner of war, it was first performed in a prisoner of war camp. Scored for clarinet, violin, piano and cello, the premiere was preceded by a theological discussion of its significance, for the composer was a devoted Roman Catholic. Messiaen was also highly aware of the colour of music. Of course, generations of composers had talked about colour, but Messiaen said that he could *visualise* the colours of different chords. His *Les Couleurs du Cité Céleste* (1963) sets out to show the colours

> Synaesethesia is another Modernist device; the exploration of links between different senses and between different artistic media.

evident in the description of the heavenly city given in the biblical apocalypse of St John (often called the Book of Revelations). He tended to write long slow pieces with no barlines, building upon Stravinsky's work on rhythm. But where the *Rite of Spring* was famous for its frequent changes of time signature, in Messiaen's work the time signature ceases to exist, creating the feeling that we are listening to music outside of a temporal framework.

Messiaen was a famous teacher of composition and one of his pupils, **Pierre Boulez** (b. 1925), was part of a generation that rediscovered the aesthetic of Anton Webern and set out to try to apply the rules of Serialism not just to pitches but to every aspect of composition, creating total Serialism. His *Le Marteau sans Maître* sets poems by René Char to music using an instrumentation that has been compared both to Schoenberg's *Pierrot Lunaire* and the jazz ensembles of the 1950s, but which also reflects a gamelan sound, reminding us of Debussy. In a similar vein, **Piet Mondrian** (1872–1944) declared that he was concerned with the logical development of Cubism, which he believed Picasso and Braques had failed to pursue.

However, while composition seemed to be acquiring more and more rules, other composers came to the fore who adopted a very different approach. **John Cage** (1912–1992) was among those who argued that composition was becoming too prescriptive and that the performers ought to be given a larger role in determining what the final sound of the performance or recording should be. Accordingly, some composers introduced elements of chance and choice to their work. Performers might be given a set of passages to play that were clearly scored, but it was up to them to choose the order in which to play them.

> It is interesting to note that where Stockhausen took Cage's aleatoric (even Dadaist) music in his stride, Boulez was profoundly unhappy with the betrayal of the total Serialism of the day.

More bewilderingly, performers were sometimes given a score which was a drawing, or which mingled notation with scribbles, with something that looked like frames from a cartoon. It was up to them to consider what the musical implications of the lines on the page might be.

> Cathy Berberian's *Stripsopedia* is not only great fun to look; it is interesting how quickly the reader begins to form a view on which signs seem to indicate which sounds.

Sometimes Modernism in 20th-century music expresses itself in the composition of concertos for instruments which were sidelined by the Romantics. The last hundred years have been a golden age for horns, violas and cellos. Similarly, trombones, tubas, euphoniums, percussion, double basses and various other previously neglected instruments have been given more varied repertoires. This reflects more than one motive:

- The exploration of individuality: a less well-known instrument creates the sense of an individual sound rather than adherence to a tradition
- The creation of new sounds: the composer may feel freer to create his own individual sound when approaching a less well-trodden path like a percussion concerto rather than a violin concerto
- The investigation of extremes: bass instruments tended to be ignored by Romantic composers because of the problems of balance and acoustics.

Picasso himself experimented in sculpture, but it was the almost three-dimensional geometry of his paintings that **Henry Moore** (1898–1986) took as his point of departure. Moore's figures combined the features of the human body with those of the landscape, and with the natural shapes of stone itself in a new kind of sculpture that was as challenging as anything Modernism had proferred, but was nevertheless emotionally arresting. There was also a strangely Romantic quality about it, since in his reclining women, for example, we seem to see human beings put back into harmony with the natural world, as the body is approximated to a row of hills and a limestone cave.

> At the same time Barbara Hepworth was developing an individual sense of form which draws on the idea that the face, as well as the body, can be a landscape.

Later artists continued the Modernist debate on what art really was: its materials and subjects, and the role of the artist in society. **Jackson Pollock** (1912–1956) became famous for the way he attacked the canvas. He moved away from the tradition of painterly care in brushwork, instead throwing and dripping paint, drawing on primitive traditions of drip painting. Like Marcel Duchamp's famous urinal, exhibited with the terse title *Fountain* (1917), Pollock's works challenge our received ideas of beauty (and of painterly technical skill) and force us to react to works not only as aesthetic objects. The stormy canvasses that resulted bear witness to a kind of frenzy on the part of the painter, and show the confidence and recklessness with which he painted.

Historians of Romanticism tend to talk about the way it split into two or more strands, and that it had early and late phases. I believe that we are too close to Modernism as a cultural phenomenon for a fully objective assessment. But perhaps when the dust settles, we will be able to see that something similar happened with Modernism, and that what we have sketched in this chapter as developments after Modernism were actually Modernism dividing into different schools, expressing in effect a shift from early Modernism to late.

7
Further perspectives

One key question that has been lurking in the background since the Preface has been whether Modernism is best understood as a development of Romanticism or as a movement which actively subverts its paradigms. Our understanding of the relationship between these movements depends in part on the art form we are studying and the provenance of the art. In Britain, Modernism looks like a subversive force, in France it seems much more like a natural development of continental Romantic principles. If you are studying French music or poetry, the journey from Saint-Saëns through Debussy to Messiaen and Boulez (or from Hugo through Baudelaire to Rimbaud and Mallarmé then Valéry and Char), although challenging, is more readily comprehensible than that from Elgar through Vaughan Williams to Birtwistle. The transition from Tennyson through Housman to Eliot is even more confusing, since so much later poetry looks a lot more like Housman's than like Eliot's.

Like Romanticism, Modernism launched an attack on its opponents, and the enemies of both included mediocrity in the arts and intellectual laziness in audiences and readerships: that far Baudelaire and Pound were in agreement. But the question remains: did Romanticism tend to bring a more heroic and affirming message to the arts, while Modernism sought out evidence of human fallibility?

Themes

When you apply the lessons learnt here to other 20th- and 21st-century work, look for and think about the following themes and motifs:

- Attack
- Shock
- Sexuality
- Extremes
- Criticising the audience, reader or viewer
- Questioning and redefining the art form itself
- Redefining recent tradition by invoking older or foreign styles
- New materials, subjects, sounds, ensembles, instrumentations.

It is also worth researching further practitioners of Modernist principles to complement those already covered.

Literature

Ezra Pound's *Hugh Selwyn Mauberley* (1920) is a disturbingly tragicomic poem in which the literary life of the early-20th century is depicted and parodied, and the meaningless destruction of the First World War is mourned. Pound launched the concept of Imagism, a poetic school that emphasises the immediacy, visual quality and arresting force of poetry. Pound's later political support for Mussolini, work on *The Cantos*, and his long spell in prison and mental hospital, contrasts deeply with Eliot's later attachment to the Church. Accordingly, Pound's work is still not as widely read and praised as it deserves to be, yet it is mystifying, powerful and funny.

Nevertheless, in *The Cantos* Pound explicitly set out to write a modern epic, a long poem which deals with personal experience, public policy and the nature of nationhood. In old age, Pound declared it to be a failure, an assemblage not a construction, and thus not a work of art. Certainly its mixture of Chinese history, Renaissance art and the economic policies of the earlier American presidents is an unusual combination. But the passionate way in which it treats its subject (perhaps one could sum it up as 'the purpose of art and the nature of society') means that it makes for very lively reading despite its difficulties. Sadly, its size, allusiveness and density have prevented it acquiring many readers, as has been the fate of Joyce's *Finnegans Wake*, which has remained largely the preserve of university study.

Baudelaire, Brecht, most Rilke and some Valéry are possible to translate fairly well into English; if you attempt to reach back to Rimbaud and Mallarmé and have no French, you won't find English verse translations get you very far.

The Poem Itself (150 European poems translated and analysed), ed. Stanley Burnshaw, Penguin 1964, is a good place to start. Michael Hamburger's *The Truth of Poetry* (Carcanet) could almost be regarded as its companion volume.

Music

Debussy's *Jeux* was first performed in Paris in 1913 and, owing to the scandal surrounding the *Rite of Spring*, which was premiered in the same city in the same year, it has never received the attention it deserves. The story concerns a night-time game of tennis between two girls and a boy, with all the flirtation that might imply. The polytonal music is characterised by unpredictable rhythms and the unfolding use of musical cells or motifs that one might expect from the composer of the earlier *Prélude à L'Après midi d'un faune* (1894; see page 25). Debussy is accordingly usually labelled an Impressionist and sometimes omitted from accounts of Modernism. Kurtág, Ligeti, Britten and Lutosławski also merit further study; consider how Neoclassicism and Minimalism fit into the story of Modernism's development.

The visual arts

There are many other painters in this period whose work would inform an analysis of Modernism; among these are de Kooning, Kokoschka, Modigliani, Klee and Dalí. For an introduction to Modernist sculpture look at Brancusi, Giacometti and Gaudier-Brzeska, whom Pound greatly admired. In terms of film, Buñuel is a key figure in the Surrealist movement and Mies van der Rohe and le Corbusier were the leading exponents of Modernist architecture.

Resources

There is an enormous amount of secondary literature on Modernism. Hugh Kenner and Paul Griffiths have written several useful books on literature and music respectively. John Berger is excellent on Picasso. Mary Acton's *Learning to look at Modern Art* is accessible; Otto Karolyi's *Introducing Modern Music* is good on technicalities, but does assume musical literacy.

Specialist ensembles such as the UK's London Sinfonietta, Germany's Ensemble Moderne and France's Ensemble Intercontemporain have all performed and recorded many of the Modernist masterpieces and the later works which they spawned. Galleries with large collections of Modernist art include London's Tate Modern and Paris' Picasso Museum.

From margins to mainstream

Some works, such as Berg's violin concerto, have just about achieved standard repertoire status, in the way that Mahler's symphonies did a generation before, and it looks as though other major Modernist pieces might enter the canon alongside Mozart, Beethoven and the usual suspects. In general, there is now much more understanding of the art works created in the great 20th-century cultural experiment. This growing understanding does, however, co-exist alongside a strong lobby that continues to insist that art works should conform to the expectations of an 1870 audience. There have long been bigots on both sides. Some rejected Benjamin Britten as too modern and ugly, others because he was too old-fashioned and out of touch. The young Stravinsky was booed by audiences as an avant-garde fraud; the old Stravinsky was booed by Pierre Boulez as a conservative fraud persisting in a lifelong failure to come to terms with the Second Viennese School.

For some people, the arts are supposed to represent an escape from life, a refuge. Modernism's concern with addressing the erotic, the violent and the irrational, its mixture of personal confession and political attack, its startling spiritual insight and sexual frankness, can be simply too much for the complacent observer who prefers to find reassurance in less challenging work. Others become overexcited by the intellectual demands that Modernism appears to present, and go about collecting sources to illuminate even the most obscure reference.

Following up those *Waste Land* notes is only the beginning: take a look at the work done on *Ulysses* or, worse, *Finnegans Wake*!

Some converts despise anything that doesn't present them with grinding dissonance, violent politics, extreme sexual appetites, impenetrably complex structures, forbiddingly dense note clusters, word games or impasto colour collisions. But Modernist works of art aren't there to replace and deny the past: on the contrary, they can take us continually back into the history and tradition with which they are in dialogue. Listen to Schoenberg, and you will be taken back to Beethoven's orchestral writing and Bach's keyboard music with a fresh perspective. Joyce should give you new reasons to read Ibsen, Flaubert and Homer; Eliot will lead you to Augustine, Pope, Shakespeare, Dante and Baudelaire. Picasso's studies of other artists are reasons in themselves to find out about the paintings by which he was inspired.

Modernism will also offer you a frame of reference for examining recent innovative work, leading to Tracey Emin, James MacMillan, Richard Rogers, Thomas Adès, Don DeLillo and Paul Muldoon. A real understanding of Modernist works both opens new doors into the past, and throws light upon an artistic future, which will continue to reinvent, retranslate and innovate.